"The book is a lot like the author—humble and unassuming. Yet after reading the book (as well as meeting the author), you find you've been moved powerfully and challenged immensely."

DAVID JONES
Missions pastor, Cross Points Church, Kansas City

"Joe and Judi Portale's testimony of pioneering the ministries of Youth With A Mission in the French world in the 1970s and beyond is the perfect guide for a new generation of missions leaders, particularly those who have a calling to go to the frontiers. . . . This inspiring story is also a gift of wisdom from an older movement to the new pioneers of global ministries far beyond the structure of Youth With A Mission."

JOHN DAWSON
President, Youth With A Mission (YWAM)

"A book by Joe Portale on pioneering is a strategic 50th birthday gift for YWAM as a movement. For movements as well as people, age can bring fading memories. Yet short memories breed shortsightedness. To release a new generation of leaders and pioneers to take YWAM into the future, the stories of our origins and the principles of pioneering must be passed on. With his own tales of trailblazing from Europe into Africa and beyond, Joe helps young pioneers to see their way to go where few have gone before."

JEFF FOUNTAIN
Former director, YWAM Europe

"What one sees and experiences in interaction with the Portales is a consistent, single-minded 'plodding,' fiercely clinging to the principles that they have learned from the Bible as well as listening to and obeying God in their personal experience. . . . As Joe points out in *Taking On Giants*, success in pioneering is making sure you've heard God clearly and making sure you obey Him completely. It's that simple. No froth, no bubble, no hype—just raw, unquestioning obedience to the word of the Lord."

DANNY LEHMANN
Dean of College of Christian Ministries, University of the Nations

"Joe Portale is the real deal—a missionary pioneer in an age when too many have become soft and demanding. . . . You will learn much from his story. Your life will be changed. You will love this b

Aut

RS
tor

D1506583

"*Taking On Giants* is terrific reading. . . . This book should be must reading for students or people doing outreach in a different nation with a different culture."

ENID SCRATCH (MAMA DAR)
Mother of YWAM cofounder Darlene Cunningham

"I don't know of anyone more steadfast and committed to a task than Joe Portale, and it's that gift that makes him a true pioneer. He has much to teach us through the principles he has learned, and the stories he teaches them through will keep you spellbound."

AL AKIMOFF
Founder, YWAM Slavic Ministries

"When Joe and Judi Portale joined a small group of students at a School of Evangelism in Lausanne, Switzerland, none of them could have dreamt that they were in the early days of a massive global movement. They absorbed the foundational values of YWAM and have walked in those values for more than forty years. In this book, Joe draws on those forty years of experience to reinforce the primary values that undergird this world-changing movement. I highly recommend it for those who want to live the adventure of pioneering in God's kingdom!"

LYNN GREEN
International chairman, Youth With A Mission

"Joe Portale was one of my first leaders in YWAM in 1974, and I held down the fort for him in Switzerland when he took the teams across the Sahara. His stories about pioneering are not only amazing; they are full of wisdom about how to start new ministries—and how not to! (Hint: avoid certain trees in the Sahel.) Seriously, this book is a must-read."

DR. TOM BLOOMER
International provost, University of the Nations

"My friend Joe Portale has literally put his life on the line to pioneer certain kinds of ministry into certain areas of the world. I have watched for over forty years as this man has lived out practically the principles we all teach. He has persevered through amazing difficulty, ambiguity, and with amazing diligence. We will never serve the needs of the world adequately without following the history of modern pioneers like Joe and his family."

DEAN SHERMAN
Former Dean, College of Christian Ministries, University of the Nations

TAKING ON
GIANTS

*A Pioneer Missionary's Pursuit
of God's Vision for Ministry and Life*

JOE PORTALE

FOREWORDS BY LOREN CUNNINGHAM AND DARLENE CUNNINGHAM

YWAM
PUBLISHING
P.O. BOX 55787   SEATTLE, WA 98155

YWAM Publishing is the publishing ministry of Youth With A Mission. Youth With A Mission (YWAM) is an international missionary organization of Christians from many denominations dedicated to presenting Jesus Christ to this generation. To this end, YWAM has focused its efforts in three main areas: (1) training and equipping believers for their part in fulfilling the Great Commission (Matthew 28:19), (2) personal evangelism, and (3) mercy ministry (medical and relief work).

For a free catalog of books and materials, call (425) 771-1153 or (800) 922-2143. Visit us online at www.ywampublishing.com.

Taking On Giants:
A Pioneer Missionary's Pursuit of God's Vision for Ministry and Life
Copyright © 2010 by Joseph Portale III

14 13 12 11 10   1 2 3 4 5

Published by YWAM Publishing
a ministry of Youth With A Mission
P.O. Box 55787, Seattle, WA 98155

ISBN 978-1-57658-534-4

Library of Congress Cataloging-in-Publication Data

Portale, Joe.
  Taking on giants : a pioneer missionary's pursuit of God's vision for ministry and life / Joe Portale.
      p. cm. — (International adventures)
    ISBN 978-1-57658-534-4
    1. Portale, Joe. 2. Missionaries—French-speaking countries—Biography. 3. Missionaries—United States—Biography. 4. Youth with a Mission, Inc. I. Title.
    BV3705.P67A3 2010
    266'.02373017541092—dc22
    [B]   2010028095

Printed in the United States of America

Contents

Foreword

I FIRST met Joe Portale in 1965, and got to know him better when he joined Youth With A Mission (YWAM) full-time in 1969. I watched him grow in God and become the father of YWAM in the Francophone world.

Pioneering has a high price. Joe almost lost his life on more than one occasion in a variety of battles: disease, being lost out in the Sahara when the road was no longer visible . . . but that's all part of his story! My part is to say that God has given Joe principles for starting new ministries or new locations of ministries. He writes about principles he has learned (often the hard way) so that you who would be pioneers in God's kingdom will be able to go further, faster, and do greater things in God than he and his generation or mine have done. You, too, will learn new things to pass on to others from your own pioneering stories as you get to stand on the shoulders of those like Joe Portale and those who have gone before you.

I love pioneering. There's a thrill. There's a joy, an adventure. You never feel bored, but you often feel challenged! If you believe you are a pioneer, then make sure you are following Jesus the great Pioneer, and also others who follow Jesus. You can learn from stories of challenges or struggles faced by those who have pioneered while *not* following Jesus. Please learn from these lessons of what to avoid! Discover the ways of God from His Word and the testimonies of pioneering lives—both of failures and victories.

LOREN CUNNINGHAM
Founder, Youth With A Mission

Foreword

I HAVE just come from the YWAM 50th anniversary celebration in West Africa during which the pioneers of that region were honored. The "father" of that movement was none other than Joe Portale, and gratefulness abounded for all he did to lay the foundations of YWAM West Africa. On every hand, we heard and saw the fruit of Joe's ministry that lasts until today, thirty-five years after he began the work there. If anyone has valuable lessons to teach about pioneering, it's Joe Portale.

At the 50th event, people from thirteen countries of West Africa were there as evidence of the "fruit that remains" and the hundreds that have responded to Jesus' command to "go" with the gospel to the nations.

The principles in this book will firmly establish in your understanding *how* this can happen—what are the principles of God and the ways of God that lead to "fruit that remains"? You will laugh and cry and love God more as you read each page.

I have known Joe since April of 1965, when I met him as a young man in Las Vegas. At that time he told me of his call to Africa, and he has never wavered. You'll read in this book how he nearly lost his life—several times—in following God's call. But through Joe's obedience and perseverance, Jesus has brought life to so many!

In 1992 Joe helped me to lead a Leadership Training School in Kenya. When the Africans heard that he was coming, they rushed outside to greet him. I'll never forget the sight. They sang songs to honor him, whooped and shouted, and danced endlessly as they welcomed him into their midst. He was truly their hero warrior returning home!

DARLENE CUNNINGHAM
Cofounder, Youth With A Mission

Preface

THIS book was written with the desire to encourage Christians from all walks of life and from every nation to follow God's call on their lives through challenges and difficulties. It contains over forty years of my story during the development of Youth With A Mission (YWAM) in the French-speaking world, beginning in the 1960s.

Many important principles of pioneering new ministries have been learned through trial and error. In this book I share hard-learned principles in an adventure narrative. These principles are not limited to my experience or the experience of YWAM, because they involve not only what we do but what attitude of heart we do it with. It is my hope that you will learn to walk more closely with God, follow His ways, and defeat the "giants" in your Promised Land, whether you are initiating and establishing new ministries or entering your life's vocation.

God has a plan and vision for what He wants to do in every people, sphere of society, and nation. We each must discover and implement His vision for our specific callings. Because Scripture plays an important part in discerning what God is saying to us at specific times, I have included numerous scriptures in this book to show how God led me and YWAM at times of decision. God speaks to us when we seek Him in faith.

Often we learn from someone else's victories and mistakes, so I have shared in this story both the ups and downs of my ministry. In the appendices you will find pioneering principles applied in a practical missions approach. If you are involved in pioneering new ministries, I encourage you to take the time to read these and explore how they might apply to your circumstances.

Join me in this adventure as we learn together to follow God into uncharted territory.

Acknowledgments

MANY people have had a part in the unfolding of this book. I would first of all like to thank Loren and Darlene Cunningham, from whom the vision of youth in missions originated. Their commitment to trusting young people made it possible for so many of us to realize our dreams. Thank you.

I especially want to thank my wife, Judi, as well as my three children, Lisa, Joseph, and Daniel, who lived through these adventures with me. I would also like to acknowledge my daughters-in-law, Michelle and Kimberly, along with my grandchildren, Samantha and Luke, who have lived these adventures in story form.

Thanks also to all those (named and unnamed in this book) who walked through these stories and lived this adventure with me. You have been "comrades in arms."

Thanks also to Janice Rogers, who directed the first Author's Training School I attended in Texas, and who encouraged me to begin putting these stories in writing.

Thank you, Scott and Sandi Tompkins, for your invaluable help to me in the writing of this book and then the many hours you invested in editing it. Thank you to the Writers Group in Kona who regularly critiqued my work and pushed me hard toward excellence.

Thank you to Ryan Davis at YWAM Publishing, who walked with me through the final editing of this book.

I can't complete this list without especially thanking God—Father, Son, and Holy Spirit—for continually inspiring and guiding me through these adventures as well as in the recording of them. Without Him none of these things would have ever happened.

Lost in the Sahara

T H E stark beauty of the Sahara surrounded our little caravan of seven Volkswagen vans as we drove south from Tamanrasset, Algeria. It would take six days to reach the next oasis in Agadez, Niger, where we would find our next supply of fuel and water. Thirty-nine of us from three missionary training schools were driving down from Europe to assist some of the needy of West Africa. In Niger our teams would head in separate directions. My Swiss team would drive southwest to minister to French-speaking Africans. But now, being in the middle of the rugged desert, West Africa seemed a long way away.

As we headed toward Niger, I became anxious by what we encountered. There was no longer a clearly defined track. The "road," indicated by tall posts planted upright every mile and a half, crossed a wide sea of sand. At each post I could faintly see the next marker on the line of the horizon. I knew if we traveled after sundown, we could easily miss a marker and get lost. Even if we found our way again, we risked using up our fuel and water before reaching the next oasis. The possibility of getting lost, and the terrible consequences of that, weighed on me heavily, making me feel like one of the overloaded camels I had seen. I was responsible for these students and staff on Youth With A Mission's first outreach to these parts of French-speaking Africa. They were depending on me as their leader.

As these thoughts raced through my head, I corrected myself. *No, Lord, they are depending on You. We all are. Please get us safely across this huge desert and into West Africa.* We had decided to make this crossing because we felt God had specifically led our school to minister in Africa following our three-month lecture phase in Europe. In prayer before the start of the school in October 1974, He had assured us that this vision was His, not ours.

The first three days out of Tamanrasset were a perpetual battle against sand traps, light-colored patches of soft sand in which vehicles sank to their axles and became firmly stuck. The faster we drove, the less likely we were to bog down. One day six vehicles got caught at the same time. It took us the entire afternoon to dig them out. We couldn't afford to lose that much time or fuel again; we would be at risk of not reaching our destination. Carrying just enough fuel and water for those six days meant that getting lost would be disastrous. Life is short without water.

One van driver was assigned the lead and at times stopped to find road markers with binoculars. The other vans followed from a safe distance at a steady speed, tracking the cloud of dust. Sometimes spreading out six vehicles abreast, we raced over the terrain, trying to avoid the soft patches in the never-ending fields of sand.

On our fourth day of travel out of Tamanrasset, we crossed into Niger, where the desert spread before us like a large beige blanket. I stared through my dust-streaked windshield, searching for a track through the desert. My vehicle occasionally shuddered and churned sand as it struggled to keep from getting caught.

For quite a while on our fifth day out I hadn't seen any markers, but I didn't give it much thought, since I was following the lead vehicle. Two hours later, driving down a slight slope, we stopped at a dead end. A large field of thirty- to forty-foot sand dunes blocked our way. All the vehicles halted in a line. I walked up to the lead vehicle and asked the driver, Keith, "What happened? Where's the track?"

"I don't know. We're lost! The last few marker posts have fallen and disappeared under the sand. I saw faint vehicle tracks, forking left and right, so I followed one of the tracks. The more forks I came to, the more confused I got. Now I don't know where we are."

My thoughts raced. "We have to find a way back to the road. If we could see the open desert, maybe we could tell the way. But we can't see anything from down here."

Keith and I laboriously trudged up the sand dune in front of us and looked around. The hills in front of us stretched out of sight. The wavy line of the horizon meant more dunes beyond it. I looked west and saw a slim corridor of flat ground where the sand dunes ended.

"The horizon over there is flat," I said. "That must be the way." Keith agreed, and we climbed down the dune.

When we reached the desert floor, two Tuareg boys, desert nomads, came out from among the sand dunes, waving to us. They didn't speak English or French, but the older one, gesturing with his hands, seemed to be asking us where we were going. I turned an imaginary steering wheel and pointed west, smiling. The boy dug his toes into the sand, indicating more soft sand in that direction. Then he faced east and pointed the opposite direction to what Keith and I had chosen. Could God have sent this boy to show us the way?

TWO

Calling and Preparation

MY DREAMS of African missions started when I was a child in Cleveland, Ohio. At a time when other boys dreamed of being cowboys, I would ride my tricycle—my older sister Ann on the back—pretending to drive a Jeep through the jungles to reach a distant tribe with the gospel.

Our church's annual mission convention fueled these youthful dreams. Missionaries came back from overseas wearing colorful national costumes, telling amazing stories, and displaying all kinds of artifacts from strange places. These people were my heroes. I heard many stories of God helping missionaries in miraculous ways. Stories of Africa—with its strange-sounding places, tribes, and languages—thrilled me most. Africa was so far away from my home and seemed so far out of reach. I knew I wanted to work there some day.

At nine, the thought of seeing real lions in Africa didn't make me afraid, but for months I was terrified by nightmares and horrible apparitions. One particular night left an indelible mark on my life. Before

I went to bed that humid mid-July night in 1956, my mother read me Bible stories about Jesus. After she left the room, I looked around in the dark, trying to distinguish shapes. As I stared at the furnishings, they stirred to life. I caught my breath in fear and yanked the covers over my head and closed my eyes, hoping for sleep. Mercifully, it came quickly. Waking in fear some time later, I could see shapes moving. Grotesque faces with hollow eyes formed before my gaze and flew at me. Animal shapes mingled with the faces. Even though I closed my eyes, they wouldn't go away.

Suddenly I remembered what my Sunday school teacher told us to do when we were afraid, and I cried out, "Jesus . . . Jesus . . . Jesus . . . ." What happened next I can hardly believe even today. As I looked past the end of my bed, the forms disappeared as the room filled with a bright light. I sat upright, wide awake. Then the room faded away, and I was traveling through a sea of bright, vivid blue, more vibrant than anything I had ever seen. In a clear blue sky above the blue-green earth, Jesus beckoned me to come. I felt myself drawn to Him. Resting there in His presence, I felt I could stay forever. I don't remember hearing any words; I just *knew* what He wanted to communicate. He wanted me to be a missionary someday.

About two and a half months later, my fourth grade teacher asked the class to write a composition about what we wanted to be when we grew up. Remembering what Jesus had shown me, I wrote that I would go to Europe to learn French. Then I would drive down to West Africa to be a missionary. When the teacher read my composition to the whole class the next day, a new resolve grew in my heart. I would do it, no matter what.

When I was fourteen, my family moved from Cleveland, Ohio, to San Jose, California. In junior high and high school my Christian life became mechanical and my early encounter with Jesus almost forgotten. But deep down inside I still knew I was supposed to be a missionary, and I took two years of junior high French and three years of high school French along with college prep courses to prepare for Bible school.

For a short period in high school, I walked away from the Lord, but my teenage rebellion didn't last long. One evening I came to my senses. *I'm called to be a missionary. Fighting against God is foolish,* I thought. So during my senior year, when I heard about a group called Youth With A Mission that was doing a one-week evangelism outreach in Las Vegas, Nevada, during Easter vacation, I signed up to go. Soon I wished I hadn't. People in Las Vegas slammed the door in my face at almost every house I went to. One positive memory I retained from the outreach was meeting Loren and Darlene Cunningham, the directors of the ministry. Their excitement about God and evangelism was infectious. My first experience with Youth With A Mission left me with something I couldn't shake off.

In the fall I entered Bethany Bible College in California. My first year I lived in the men's dorm. I had several classes with one of my dorm mates, Al Akimoff. He told me about his short-term mission work in the Bahamas during the previous two summers with Youth With A Mission (he referred to it as YWAM, pronouncing it "why-wam"). I told him about my not-so-good experience witnessing door-to-door with YWAM in Las Vegas. Al smiled and acknowledged that some places could be very difficult, but said I shouldn't give up because of that. He talked with such excitement about seeing God intervene in people's lives and told me stories of miracles they had seen while witnessing in the Bahamas. I didn't yet share his enthusiasm for YWAM, but that year Al and I became close friends.

One evening near the end of my first semester, I sat at a large cafeteria table with two awkward fellows who were discussing the evils and absurdities of social interaction with girls. As I ate my meal and listened halfheartedly, I noticed a girl come into the cafeteria. She hung up her mid-length, buff-colored corduroy coat, looked around the room, and then headed to the food line. Her short, brown hair bounced as she walked, and her smile radiated an air of self-confidence. *I wouldn't mind meeting her,* I thought. Out of the corner of my eye, I saw her get her meal and then walk toward where I was sitting. She sat down just to my left, said grace, and began to eat her dinner.

The two fellows, still in conversation about the evils of social interaction, turned and asked me whether I thought holding hands with a girl was evil. Absentmindedly, I nodded my agreement, wondering how I could start up a conversation with this girl to my left. All of a sudden she spoke. "That's the most ridiculous thing I've heard in my whole life," she declared, going on to take a stand for normal social interaction and having fun. Her hazel-green eyes sparkled through the debate. When the discussion dwindled off, she picked up her tray and left. I was intrigued by her and by the fact that she was willing to stand up for what she believed and could express what she thought. I soon learned her name was Judi Huffman, and I had the opportunity to speak to her a few times in the cafeteria and library.

A few weeks later I asked Judi to go with me to a youth rally, and she agreed. I was nervous when I picked her up, but as we began the scenic drive across the Santa Cruz mountains, Judi put me at ease with her contagious smile and disarming sense of humor. Her self-confident and relaxed air helped me relax. I could be myself.

Our friendship grew during our second year of college. We often studied together in the library after dinner. Every time I saw Judi, it brightened my day. When I was with her, I could be honest and open, and she was open with me as well. I began to ask the Lord if this was the person I should spend the rest of my life with. Before letting our relationship progress to that point, however, I had to talk to her about my calling to missions and Africa. It wouldn't be fair to propose marriage and then get her involved in a mission commitment that she was unprepared for.

One day, after praying for the right moment, I met her outside the girls' dorm. "Judi, I need to talk to you about something very important." I continued slowly. "I have a call to be a missionary, probably to French-speaking Africa. Do you have a missionary calling?"

Judi smiled. "Yes, I have a missionary calling, though I've never thought of Africa. But I'm open to whatever God has for me."

I was relieved. The idea of serving overseas didn't seem like a big deal to Judi. Now I felt that I could pursue our relationship seriously without compromising either Judi's or my life's calling.

I secretly bought an engagement ring, and on December 9, 1966, I asked Judi to marry me. She didn't say yes immediately, pointing out that I hadn't asked her dad for permission yet. So after dinner we drove to her parents' home. By the time we arrived, it was very late, and Judi's father, a former Marine, was already in bed asleep. I breathed a sigh of relief, thinking I had a reprieve. But to my horror I watched Judi march into her parents' bedroom, wake up her father, and announce, "Joe has something to ask you, Dad." My heart started beating so loudly that I could hear it thumping in my ears.

About a minute later Judi's father emerged from the bedroom, looked at me sleepily, and waited for me to speak. I tried to clear the lump from my throat two or three times, but no words came out. The look on his face seemed to say, *I would like to be in bed right now.* I finally blurted out, "I, uh, want to ask your permission, uh, to have Judi's hand in marriage."

He smiled, and with that assurance the thumping of my heart in my ears began to fade. "Oh, is that what you wanted, Joe? Of course I give you my permission. Congratulations to both of you. Now, can I go back to sleep?"

I took a deep breath and let it out. "Sure. Uh, thank you. Good night."

Judi smiled. "Thank you, Dad."

Judi and I headed out the door and drove back to the college. On the way Judi leaned over to me and smiled. "Now it's official. We're engaged."

One particular day in Bible college etched itself indelibly in my mind. It dawned bright and clear, with the pungent fragrance of autumn among the redwood trees, but I couldn't enjoy it. I was on my way to give my first sermon in homiletics class, where we studied the art of preaching. I knew this skill would help me immensely in my missionary work. Each student was to prepare and persuasively preach three sermons during the semester that were then critiqued by the teacher and students. The problem was, I was not a preacher. I could teach a small Sunday school class, but public speaking had always been difficult for me. And yet I could not escape it. After Bible college I had to successfully serve as senior pastor of a church for two years before applying for missionary appointment with my denomination. That meant I would have to preach every Sunday morning and evening and every Wednesday night for two years.

As I slowly walked up the hill to my classroom, I mentally reviewed my sermon's introduction and three-point outline. I had put a lot of time into preparing it, but I knew I might forget everything when I started to preach. I quietly slipped into the small, window-lit classroom and found a place to sit halfway back. I flashed a weak smile at my buddy Al Akimoff who was seated across from me. My stomach and mind churned too hard to try to make conversation.

When I heard my professor say, "Joe, come up and give your sermon now," I walked to the front of the room. My mind and body seemed to spin out of control. My heart started to pound noisily in my ears and throat. My voice would not cooperate. I cleared my throat several times. My knees were weak. With a wavering voice, I opened with prayer, as I had been taught to do. "Dear God, I ask You, Lord, to come and help us, Lord, to learn from You, Jesus, from this chapter, Lord, in the book of John, Lord. In Jesus' name, amen."

By this time my ears were ringing and my head was feeling light. I wondered if the class was as distracted as I was by my intense breathing. I had to hang on. I opened my Bible and read my text. The pages stuck to my perspiring hands. I desperately struggled not to lose my place. Somehow with the help of my notes I was able to get through my three-point outline and reach my conclusion. Only eight minutes had passed, but my body ached like I had preached for two hours.

While I remained up front, the professor called on a student in the front row of the classroom to comment on my sermon. He began, "Joe, I think that you did a good job, Joe, of covering your subject, Joe. But I think, Joe, that you need to be more careful, Joe, how you pray, Joe. You don't need to mention God's name, Joe, so many times, Joe, when you pray." The class burst into laughter and my face flushed. I wanted to respond, "But I tried. I gave you a sermon—comment on that." But those words would not come out. I just stood there and looked at him in bewilderment.

After class I walked out of the room and grabbed hold of Al, trying to get some encouragement. He mumbled, "That's okay, Joe. You win some and lose some." I felt confused, humiliated, inadequate, and hurt.

Crowds of students pushed past me as I walked down the hill to my next class. *What in the world am I doing here preparing for the ministry? I don't fit the mold. Am I trying to do the wrong thing? How can I fulfill my dream of being a missionary if I can't even preach a sermon to my classmates?* My thoughts flickered back to my childhood and to that eventful night, at nine years of age, when Jesus called me to be a missionary. It had been so real then. Even though that experience was such a long time ago, it was still an anchor for me. *I have to keep trying, even though I can't preach. I'm called to be a missionary.*

Although I didn't know what my future as a missionary would look like, I did know one thing: I wouldn't be alone. After an eight-month engagement, Judi and I married in August 1967. I was twenty and she was nineteen. We rented a little pink, one-bedroom house perched between several tall redwood trees, right on campus between the men's and women's dorms. It took both of us to meet our living expenses. Judi, who had stopped taking classes to earn money for our wedding, worked in town to help pay for my tuition, and I worked every afternoon at a cabinet shop.

Things unraveled the first morning after our wedding. Going to brush my teeth, I found that Judi had squeezed my neatly arranged toothpaste tube in the middle. Straightening my demolished tube, I returned it to the shelf. *She can see it and figure out what to do,* I thought. But this continued daily for a couple of weeks. Exasperated, I finally voiced my concern. Judi laughed. When I didn't laugh in return, she looked confused. "Are you serious, Joe?"

"Why, yes, of course. I was taught there's only one way to squeeze toothpaste."

"You gotta be kidding me," she reacted.

"Please try," I mumbled, and left the room.

As the days went by, I kept straightening out the toothpaste tube each morning. Then one day, having squeezed out the very last drop, I took the empty tube into the kitchen to throw it into the wastebasket. As I reached to toss it in, a thought came. *What's that in your hand?*

My immediate response was, *It's a piece of garbage.*

Then a startling thought popped into my head. *Then why are you putting at risk a marriage that you vowed was "till death do us part" for a piece of garbage?*

Convicted, I asked God to forgive me. Then I found Judi. "I love you and the way God made you. Please forgive me for my attitude about the toothpaste tube."

She quickly and graciously responded, "Of course I do."

During our first year of marriage I discovered that not everything in daily life had to be done the way that I had always done it. I learned to accept that Judi did things differently than I did and yet accomplished the same results. Many times I had to ask Judi's forgiveness for trying to force her into my mold. When I began to appreciate our differences rather than just tolerate them, I realized what a wonderful wife God had given me. Similarly, the apostle Paul instructed the church in Ephesus to "[bear] with one another in love" (Ephesians 4:2). This revelation was a major help to me not only in marriage but also, eventually, in cross-cultural ministry. I realized that we need people working with us who have different ways of doing things and different personalities.

One morning in my pastoral preaching class a fellow student shared his excitement at being hired by a large church. A question troubled me. Was the ultimate reward of our studies to get a good job in a large church to get a big salary? As I sat in class, I cried out in my heart, *God, if this is all the ministry is about, getting a good job with a good paycheck, I can make better money doing something else. If there is something real about the ministry, I am willing to give my whole life to it. If it's more than just a job to pay the bills, Lord, please help me discover it.*

Through all of my experiences so far, I couldn't get away from the fact that I had heard God's call on my life and that God was preparing me for ministry. I wondered what it would be and where He would lead me and my new partner next. I did not expect the answer He would give me shortly.

THREE

France: A New Horizon

JUST before Christmas 1968, during my final year of college, my buddy Al thrust a brochure into my hand and said, "Look what I just received in the mail. It's from YWAM. They're starting a School of Evangelism in Switzerland. You should consider going, Joe."

I laughed. "Al, I'm just about to complete four years of college. I have a wife, and it's time I got into the ministry. I don't need another school."

Al smiled. "Think about it, Joe. I'm considering going myself." Back at home I slipped the brochure onto my bookshelf.

Sometime later my thoughts turned to the brochure Al had given me. I pulled it out and began reading. The school was a fourteen-month "laboratory of evangelism" where youth would come for training in evangelism, language, and the ways of God. For those who had already graduated from formal training, this school would be a springboard to full-time service. It involved learning by doing, requiring a minimum of classroom training. The students were expected to become fluent in a European language, and French was one of the choices. The brochure also spoke about students traveling to the Holy Land to study the methods of Christ in evangelism at a camp on the shores of Galilee and the methods of the apostle Paul right where he preached.

All these things—learning by doing, French studies, and a study tour in the Holy Land—whetted my appetite. Could this be the door God was opening for me after Bible college, my first step toward Africa? The opportunity piqued my interest, but at the same time I felt I had had enough schooling and needed to start in ministry.

The next morning, over a bowl of cold cereal and a cup of coffee, I shared my thoughts with Judi. Her light-green eyes shined as we talked; she was eager to pursue whatever path God had for us. Our discussion continued for the next few days, but we were still undecided about what to do. I felt more and more drawn to the school in Switzerland, but I wondered how we would we pay for it. Judi puzzled over the same question.

Late one night my heart filled with hope as I finished reading a book by Brother Andrew called *God's Smuggler*, which Al had read and insisted I read too. I wondered if I could experience the same kinds of things in my life that Brother Andrew had experienced. *Could the school in Switzerland be what Judi and I are supposed to do next?* Deep down I knew that was it, and I made my decision. *We'll go to that school.*

The next morning before Judi left for work, I told her about my decision. (I hadn't yet learned to include her in final decisions, especially when they involved us both.) Mid-morning I went to my campus mailbox. Opening an envelope addressed to me, I found a fifty dollar bill inside. There was no letter, just the words "God bless you" written on the flap. This was the first time that had ever happened to me. I stood there in amazement, sensing that God was answering my plea to see Him involved in my life and confirming the decision I had made. Standing there, I heard my name paged to go to the dean of students' office.

As I entered the office, the dean introduced me to a kindly gentleman in a gray-blue suit. He was the pastor of a large church in my hometown. "I need an assistant pastor, and the dean says you would be a good candidate," he began. "I need someone to work with the youth and the Christian education department. The salary will be good."

My thoughts raced. *This church is less than a mile from my parents' home. It's the type of work I enjoy. But what about last night and the fifty dollars today? Wasn't that from God?*

"Thank you very much for this wonderful offer," I began. "But I can't accept it."

"But, Joe, the salary is very good," the pastor reassured me.

"It's not a matter of money," I said. "Last night I decided to go to this school in Europe. Then this morning I received fifty dollars in the mail. God wants to take care of me, but I need to do what He wants." Both men looked puzzled. I could tell I had really muddied the water.

I excused myself from the dean's office and walked to my next class. Opportunities like this didn't come every day, and I had burned my bridges. There were no other calls from the dean's office. Later I understood how following God's call involved giving up my rights and reputation.

Al had also decided to go to the YWAM school, as had two other couples from our class, Don and Deyon Stephens and David and Carol Boyd. Our applications were accepted. Just before graduation all seven of us agreed to meet in New York the following month and take the same charter flight to Europe.

Meanwhile, Judi and I worked and saved for the school in Switzerland. We chose not to tell anyone about our financial needs and trusted God to provide for us. Through various gifts and what we earned, we saved enough money to cover the cost of our first eight and a half months of school. But we were short the cost of the last five and a half months. Shortly before leaving for Europe, I called YWAM and explained our situation. They said if our parents agreed to pay any remaining amount at the end of the school, then we could come. I asked my parents and they agreed, releasing us to follow the call of God. However, we didn't intend to have my parents pay for us in the end; we would continue to pray about and search for ways to raise the money through other means. Judi and I sold our car to buy our plane tickets.

On the hot, humid day of June 28, 1969, Judi and I flew to JFK International Airport in New York en route to Europe. We found our way that evening to the charter terminal where our Icelandic Airlines flight would depart and were warmly greeted by the Stephenses, the Boyds, and Al. The dingy waiting room had old, yellowed linoleum on the floor, off-white walls decorated with an occasional poster, and yellow and blue vinyl chairs with arm rests that kept us from stretching across them for a nap. But our high spirits surely brightened the room.

YWAM leadership had assigned us all to teams already in ministry around Europe. We would serve for two months with these teams before heading to the school in Switzerland. Don and Deyon talked excitedly about being assigned to Germany. David and Carol would also go there. Al would go to Spain. And Judi and I would link with a team in France. This country interested me, though I still felt that tug toward Africa.

Around midnight a voice paged the boarding of our charter flight. As we gathered up our mountains of carry-on luggage and staggered to the gate, I wondered what we would discover at the other end of this flight. I could not have imagined then the gateway that was opening before us.

Our flight ended late the next day in Luxembourg, a small country in Western Europe bordering Germany, Belgium, and France. After a short night's sleep, we headed in different directions. Al traveled with Judi and me to Paris, where he would take a train to Spain to join his team. We traveled by bus, passing through quaint villages and by ancient-looking buildings and lonely farmhouses. The closer we got to Paris, the more excitement welled up in my spirit.

Hours later the bus stopped by a café in a huge city. The driver informed us we were in Paris, unloaded our suitcases, and departed. I had no idea where we were in this huge metropolitan area of over twelve million people. We were over five thousand miles from our home, and all I had was a phone number of a contact in Paris. I searched for a pay phone and in the process discovered that I couldn't understand anyone, nor could they understand me. My high school French had failed me.

After much confusion and some sign language by an obliging waiter at the corner café, I found a pay phone. To my dismay the French coins I had didn't fit. I found the waiter again and pointed toward the phone. "Telephone," I said. Showing my hand turning a dial, I held up my coins.

He got the message and said, "*Jeton, jeton*" (token, token). He pointed across the street to a newspaper stand and said, "*Kiosque*" (kiosk).

I walked over to the kiosque, said the magic word, "jeton," and held up my money. After purchasing one of these strange coins, I made my way back to the telephone. I put my jeton into the slot, pushed the red button, and dialed. The coin dropped through, but no one answered the phone. When I tried to retrieve my jeton, it didn't come out. So I walked back to the kiosque and bought two more. I tried the same procedure with the same result. I studied the writing on the phone and somehow figured out I wasn't supposed to push the red button until someone answered the phone. This assured that if no one answered, I would still have my jeton. This machine did not return jetons; it only ate them.

On my next try someone answered the phone. "*Allo?* . . . *Allo?* . . . *Allo?*" the voice kept repeating. The person couldn't hear me. Although I was pushing the red button, the jeton wouldn't drop; the connection was not going through. I finally got the jeton to drop just in time for the person on the other end to hang up the phone. I purchased two more jetons at the kiosque. Returning to the phone, I suggested that Judi and Al pray while they sat on our hard-shelled green suitcases on the side-walk outside the café. I dialed the number with my jeton poised for immediate action. The phone rang and someone answered. I pressed the red button, pushed in the jeton, and said, "Hello!"

The response came. "*Allo, qu'est ce que vous voulez?*" (What do you want?)

"Do you speak English?" I said rapidly. "I've just arrived from America, and I'm trying to find the YWAM team." Silence. "Do you speak English?" Silence. Then the phone went dead. *If I don't have the right number, I have no way to get the correct one,* I thought.

Exasperated, I went out to talk to Judi and Al about my battle. We had come too far just to turn around in defeat. Anyway, we had come on one-way tickets. We had to locate the team.

After we prayed, I went to the phone with my fifth jeton and repeated the dialing procedure. *Please, Lord. Help me get through to someone who speaks English. We don't have anywhere else to go.* The phone rang and an American-sounding voice answered, "Hello?" The red button went in, my last jeton dropped through, and my voice could be heard. During the conversation I ran outside to get the names of the streets by the café. The encouraging voice on the phone assured me that someone would be coming for us shortly by metro, and they did.

That evening Judi and I camped out in the balcony of an old movie theater used by a church in downtown Paris. The rest of the YWAM team stayed elsewhere in the building. I could hear rats scurry across the dusty floor, and every ten minutes the balcony shook as the metro rumbled through the subway below the theater. When Judi asked me what the scurrying sounds were, I assured her that it was just the metro. She relaxed and slept better than I did.

The next morning Al departed for Spain. Within a few days our team moved to a rural area in northern France to work with a missionary living in an old farmhouse with no flush toilets. The girls slept in the attic, and the boys camped in a large brown tent in a nearby field. Judi and I were one of two married couples who shared the tent with the boys. Our area was separated by old blankets hung over ropes. Privacy was nonexistent. We slept on army cots and walked on old boards to avoid the muddy, rain-soaked ground. On Saturdays we showered at a public bath house.

Beginning our work, we quickly memorized four sentences in French to use in door-to-door ministry, telling people we had Christian literature for sale. The fourth sentence flatly stated, "*Je ne parle pas le français*" (I don't speak French). Armed with this repertoire and our red-and-black plaid literature bags, we headed out.

One warm summer day the missionary dropped Judi and me off in a rural farming village. There were wide spaces between each farmhouse, and old steel-spiked fences surrounded every farmyard. Big, black, steel-barred gates supported by stone-block posts closed the farmyards off from strangers. As Judi and I proceeded to the first gate, we saw a large sign with the words CHIEN MÉCHANT. Judi looked at me and asked, "What does that mean, Joe?" I had no idea, but I remembered from high school that an accent often meant a letter had been dropped from the word. I stared at the word *méchant* (vicious). If I added an *r* next to the accent, it would make the word *merchant*. I glanced around the farmyard to get a hint as to what kind of merchant it was, and all I could see were chickens. Looking at the word *chien* (dog), I could see that by adding the letters *ck* in the middle, it would create the word *chicken*.

I quickly and proudly announced, "It's simple, Judi. It says 'chicken merchant.' You can see all his chickens in the farmyard." With a smile, Judi acknowledged my wonderful grasp of French.

I opened the gate and walked ahead of Judi into this "chicken merchant's" yard. About ten feet in I heard terrible snarling. To my right I saw a brown, short-haired dog with pit bull features charging at us, its eyes flashing with a green light. My heart pumped frantically, adrenalin flowed, and my mind instinctively told my feet what to do. Judi and I turned in unison to regain the gate before disaster struck. Thankfully, when we had entered, the gate didn't click shut behind us. With greater speed than it takes to tell, we both grabbed for that slightly ajar gate. Its hinges squeaked in protest but gave way to our frantic push. As we raced through it, I flung it backward as hard as I could. I heard the wild barking of the dog, the squeaking of the gate on its hinges, and my heart pounding in my throat. After a split second that seemed like an eternity, I heard the click of the gate into its latch, followed by a crash and more frantic barking. Judi and I stopped running and let out sighs of relief, trying to regain composure. As I listened to that dog, I could not imagine why a chicken merchant would keep such a ferocious animal!

Judi and I spent the rest of the day trying to visit "chicken merchants." At another farmyard with that same sign, Judi and I slowly backed out of the ever-appreciated steel gate while holding back two snarling dogs as they bit our plaid literature bags. I had not imagined missionary life like this. We were willing to give our lives for the gospel, but surely not this way.

A French evangelist, Marcel Tabailloux, joined us for a couple of weeks, holding evangelistic meetings in nearby towns and villages. Our team sang and testified, and Marcel showed films from Moody Bible Institute and preached. Several mornings he spoke to our team about the spiritual needs of France. He told us that out of the fifty-plus million people of France in 1969, only five to ten percent were practicing Catholics and less than one percent were Protestant. Most Frenchmen were not religious; they were rationalists. Out of the thirty-eight thousand towns in France, thirty-five thousand had no permanent gospel witness. Many French were superstitious and consulted mediums or spiritist healers. The occult was alive and well. Marcel challenged us that the key to reaching the French was to love them through prayer and witnessing. As we continued to minister to these people, we discovered a growing love in our hearts for them. We could see that France was a spiritually dry and needy country.

Although we sold many Bibles, youth materials, and children's books and saw about ten people receive Christ, the incident that I remember most is an encounter Judi and I had with an old, slightly stooped farmer. We had been going door-to-door in his village. When we arrived at his door, he could tell by our broken French and accents that we were from the United States. He invited us to sit on his front porch for a cold drink of sweetened lemonade so he could tell us his story. During World Ward II, when German forces took over his village, they took away his horse. As a farmer he was left unable to function. When the American GIs liberated his village, they returned his horse to him. He wanted us to know his story and to thank us for what those soldiers had done. After having dogs chase us out of countless "chicken merchant" farmyards, and having many people refuse our witness, it was so refreshing to have someone thank us as Americans for what some GIs had done twenty-four years earlier. We gave the man some literature before we left. It was encouraging to have someone respond positively to us during our outreach.

Near the end of the two-month summer outreach, Judi and I discussed our finances. We still owed $1,400 tuition, the equivalent of five and a half months of school fees. Within two weeks we would have to give an account of how we would pay for the rest of the school. We needed God to provide either $1,400 cash or $100 support per month for the fourteen months we would be in Europe. Wanting to trust God for our financial needs, we prayed, "Lord, we don't believe it's right for us to go into debt. If this is Your will for us to continue in this school, would You provide by the end of this summer what we need to pay our tuition in full or the monthly support to cover it? If not, we will take it that we made a mistake and You do not really want us here."

About ten days later someone brought our team mail. Judi and I had several letters. One from my parents said our home church had decided to support us $50 per month, and a couple from our church had decided to send us $25 per month. Both had already begun donating this amount through YWAM. Then we opened a letter from my uncle, who was the pastor of another church. He wanted to send us $25 per month and had already begun sending it to YWAM. God had provided exactly what we needed! *We must be right where He wants us to be,* I thought. A growing assurance welled up in my spirit.

FOUR

Learning to Walk in God's Ways

AT THE end of the summer, all the teams came to Lausanne, Switzerland, for one week of reporting. From there we separated for four months, going to French, German, and Spanish language schools in Switzerland and Germany. Judi and I studied French in Lausanne along with twelve other "YWAMers," as YWAM missionaries were called. Loren Cunningham asked me to be responsible for that group. We enrolled in a professional language school and were lodged in the homes of French-speaking families.

Designed to teach spoken French through the immersion method, the school was extremely challenging. It taught French in French. Judi, who had never studied the language before, burst into tears several times after class. "I know my teacher speaks English, but she won't. I just don't understand," she cried. We saw the effectiveness of this method later, when Judi and I were conversant in French by the end of the school.

A couple who had dropped out of the School of Evangelism (SOE) stayed to attend the same language school. The husband continually criticized YWAM, and slowly his attitude seeped into my spirit. I found myself reacting to people and problems by complaining and criticizing. I knew my attitude was affecting others, but I made no effort to change. I was here to learn to converse in French, and that was that, I thought. In fact, my attitude would play a large part in what I would learn during the SOE.

The language courses ended on December 20, 1969, and all the SOE students returned to Lausanne for the three-month lecture portion of our school, held in an old hotel YWAM had rented. It was good to see Al, the Boyds, the Stephenses, and the twenty other students. The day after Christmas school began in earnest. Each month Christian leaders came for one or two weeks to teach from their practical experience about the ways of God. As we learned more about the character of God, I began to see that His love is the foundation of it. All that God is and does is defined by His love (1 John 4:8, 16).

I was especially challenged by the teaching of Joy Dawson. This intercessor from New Zealand knew God and had a powerful teaching and prophetic gift. She prodded us to know God intimately, learn to walk in His ways, and seek Him for direction in our lives. One of the ways of walking with God had to do with our tongue. "Always pass on something good about someone else, never anything negative," Joy said. I recognized how criticism had a major impact on our spiritual lives and how I needed to grapple with this area, but I wasn't quite sure how. Or maybe I wasn't yet willing to admit what I understood.

One day Joy encouraged us to ask God to show us the roots of our heart. I wondered if God really spoke to His children directly. If he did, I wanted to experience it. So that night I prayed that God would give me a revelation of my heart. When I didn't sense anything, I thought to myself, *Oh well. I guess that's that.* A few days later Joy gave us a homework assignment. Without using a concordance, we were to ask God to show us a passage in the Bible that spoke to us personally of His greatness. Then we were to write out areas where we needed to make adjustments relating to what God said. This gave me another opportunity to see if hearing the voice of the Lord was for real.

I got alone with my Bible, knelt at the side of my bed, and prayed, "Lord, please guide me. I know You're willing to answer my prayer, but if there is any sin in my heart that would hinder this, please show me. I yield to Your Holy Spirit. I give You all my own ideas, and I refuse the confusions of the enemy. Where do you want me to read in the Bible about Your greatness? Please lead me." As I waited, wondering where to read, the thought came to my mind: *Psalm 104.* I sat in a chair and read verse one: "Praise the LORD, O my soul. O LORD my God, you are very great; you are clothed with splendor and majesty." Through the Psalm's vivid descriptions, I got a picture of God's greatness. A thought crossed my mind. *Could it have been God who directed me to Psalm 104 in response to my prayer? Is this His personal communication to me about His greatness?*

I continued reading. Psalm 105 showed God's greatness in His dealings with Israel. Psalm 106 continued the story of God's mighty acts. I puzzled at how Israel allowed itself to lose sight of God's greatness by complaining and doing such evil deeds in the desert. My eyes fell on verses 32 and 33. "By the waters of Meribah they angered the LORD, and trouble came to Moses because of them; for they rebelled against the Spirit of God, and rash words came from Moses' lips." A strange feeling stirred in my heart—understanding as well as sadness. Moses was trying to lead the children of Israel, who were murmuring for lack of water. God told him to speak to the rock and it would give water. In his humanness Moses got angry with Israel and struck the rock. Because of that, God told Moses he could not enter the Promised Land. I realized consequences were linked to how a spiritual leader carried out his responsibilities. Then I understood the stirring in my heart; it was a sense of sadness and disappointment in my own sin—my criticizing and complaining while I was responsible for our language school group. I recognized that I had hurt people. *Could this be the Lord communicating to me?*

The second part of our homework assignment was to apply what the Lord spoke to us. I knelt again and asked the Lord what kind of adjustments I needed to make in light of these verses. The first was obvious. I had hurt some of my friends. I didn't want to be like Moses, forbidden to enter God's Promised Land because of rash words. My spirit cried out to the Lord, asking for His mercy and forgiveness for my sin against Him and the people in my French language school.

As I waited silently in prayer, I was startled by another thought. *In class I should ask forgiveness of the entire group I offended. They were all affected by my sin.* That was not what I wanted to hear. Hear God, yes; humble myself, no. My defenses rose. *My sins are already covered by the blood of Jesus. I don't need to do anything. I don't believe in public confession.* But I could not get that idea out of my mind. When I pursued fellowship with God, the same thought came back. When I refused it, I heard only silence. I felt miserable. I didn't want to lose the joy I had in hearing God. I desperately wanted to know God better. But I certainly didn't want to confess my sin to the whole school. Finally, I prayed, "God, if this really is You, and if You want me to confess and ask forgiveness of the people I have offended in this school, then have Joy call on me at the beginning of class tomorrow and ask me if I have anything to share." I felt better after praying this. Joy's practice was to enter the classroom, open with prayer, and begin teaching. If God really had communicated with me, He had the opportunity to confirm it very practically. I was able to relax and go to bed, feeling that I had more or less resolved my dilemma.

The next morning I got up early and committed my day to the Lord. As class was about to begin, I looked out the classroom window at the snow-flocked trees and relaxed, knowing that when Joy didn't call on me, I could throw off this feeling of guilt and go on with life. Joy walked into the classroom, went up to the lectern, bowed her head, and prayed. She waited in silence for a moment to see if God wanted to speak anything to her and then said, "Amen." She lifted her head, looked over at me, and asked, "Joe, do you have anything to share with us from last night's homework assignment?" I was startled speechless. I felt uncovered, like she could see into my soul. I stood to my feet and with a lump in my throat stammered, "Uh . . . yes, I do." A sense of peace and assurance flooded me; I now knew God had spoken to me. My doubts were gone. I began describing to the class the picture God had shown me of His greatness through Psalms 104, 105, and 106. Then I shared Psalm 106:32–33. As I asked forgiveness of those I had criticized, my heart was filled with love for them. God was healing relationships as well as my heart attitude.

After class I felt so free I thought I could fly. God had not only freed me from the bondage of criticism, but He had also adjusted my theology and my understanding of forgiveness. Asking people's forgiveness when I sinned against them was a part of the healing process. And having a clean heart was not only good for me, but it was also important to God. He doesn't want preachers or teachers to move in a spirit of criticism when they minister, so being freed from a critical spirit was essential for receiving His anointing. "Thank You, God," I prayed, "You do communicate, and what You say is important to me."

And God had more to communicate to me. A particular treat for Al Akimoff and me was the week Brother Andrew came to teach. He picked up where his book *God's Smuggler* left off. Telling us what God was doing in supposedly closed countries, he shared spiritual principles necessary to make a difference. One principle was being aware of the invisible, spiritual world. To illustrate, Brother Andrew referred to Elisha and his servant in 2 Kings 6:15–17.

Elisha's servant went out early one morning and discovered the city surrounded by an enemy army. Panicked, he ran to Elisha and asked what they should do. "'Don't be afraid,' the prophet answered. 'Those who are with us are more than those who are with them.' And Elisha prayed, 'O LORD, open his eyes so he may see.' Then the LORD opened the servant's eyes, and he looked and saw the hills full of horses and chariots of fire all around Elisha." Elisha had seen the invisible world, so he was without fear. Brother Andrew looked at us and asked, "Are you tuned into the invisible world? If so, it produces visible results."

I began to understand that if I wanted to make a difference in the visible world, I had to be aware of the invisible one that influences it. "Lord," I prayed, "please open my eyes to see what You want me to see as You lead me into the future ministry You are preparing me for."

I was caught off guard by where God led me next—into the invisible world of my heart. As I prayed one day, I suddenly got a glimpse of the evil and blackness of my own heart. I couldn't believe what I saw: sins I had committed against people in my past, bitterness, hatred, lack of forgiveness, jealousy, criticism, and prideful independence. I asked the Lord for His mercy and forgiveness. I sensed that He forgave me but was also challenging me to communicate to the people I had wronged and ask for forgiveness. So began a process of writing letters of restitution to people. I realized the sin of criticism had been rooted in my life for many years. God was not only dealing with my sin but also highlighting bad habits I had developed. I needed to unlearn them and begin learning good habits, and I asked God to help me. Two days later in my regular Bible reading, God spoke to me through Isaiah 60:2. "See, darkness covers the earth and thick darkness is over the peoples, but the LORD rises upon you and his glory appears over you." I sensed the Lord saying He had heard my prayers. He was working in my life, and His presence would be with me.

Two weeks later Loren asked me to take our school to a university town in France, not far from the Swiss border, for a weekend of witnessing. I contacted a French pastor I knew, and ten days later we began witnessing on the university campuses. We wanted to evangelize in radical, youthful ways, but the local pastor insisted we use his more conservative methods. My spirit rose up with anger and criticism. But another principle warred with it, that of honoring this pastor. Thinking of what I had walked through two weeks before, I prayed, "Lord, please help me not revert back to my old habits. Help me overcome this tendency to criticize." I was able to continue working with the pastor despite our differing views on how to reach the students. To me our outreach was ineffective, but the valuable lesson I learned was worth the struggle. I had discovered a new way of affirmation and encouragement, which the Lord wanted me to walk in.

Returning to Lausanne and reflecting on that weekend, I realized the Lord had allowed what looked like a brick wall to block my path in ministry. As I called upon Him, I was able to overcome it. Over the next few months I encountered more brick walls. Sometimes I didn't realize what they were at first, and stumbled along the way. But every time I called on the Lord, He enabled me to surmount the obstacle. I began to see a pattern in God's dealings with me. The brick walls He allowed in my life became the steps of a stairway that led me to the heart attitudes necessary for the ministry He was calling me to.

I was also beginning to understand that humility was needed in cross-cultural ministry and that Christians from different cultures could learn from each other. I needed to spend time getting to know the people I ministered with and walk in cultural sensitivity. I didn't always have the complete picture; I needed to avoid the attitude of superiority and instead have a teachable spirit. Soon I would be immersed in many more cultures, and the lessons I had learned in just a few months would prove to be crucial in my ministry.

Stirring Up Hunger for God

IN THE spring of 1970 the whole school, over thirty of us, set out for the Middle East in Volkswagen vans. On our three-month study tour, we would minister in Protestant, Roman Catholic, Greek Orthodox, Jewish, Muslim, and Marxist countries. From Greece to Israel we sailed on a Jewish immigrant ship, the *Delphi,* carrying 525 passengers. On the final morning the ship buzzed with excitement. Hundreds of people stood on deck searching the horizon for their first glimpse of Israel. Suddenly someone on a top deck shouted and pointed as Mount Carmel became visible on the horizon. Rejoicing broke out on deck. People gathered at the railings, hugging each other and weeping.

It was exciting to land in Haifa, Israel, and be in this place of ancient history. Just as the brochure for the School of Evangelism had promised, we had the opportunity to study evangelism methods where Jesus walked and taught and healed. However, the country was full of people still emotionally scarred from war and persecution. They weren't very open to hearing about Jesus, but we counted it a privilege to be there, praying for them and encouraging them. Later we traveled through

41

Turkey, Greece, Bulgaria, and Romania, and went to some of the places where the apostle Paul preached.

In Greece we had a week of teaching with Duncan Campbell, a Scottish Presbyterian minister, who stirred a hunger in our hearts for prayer and intercession. He had been involved in the Hebrides revivals of the 1950s. Speaking with a strong Scottish brogue, he said, "A God-sent revival has communities gripped by the fear of the Lord." He explained that prayer is always the beginning of revival; none of the moves of God begin without it. He went on to tell us a story.

In the early 1950s he was sitting on the platform at a Christian convention near Belfast, getting ready to speak. The Lord spoke to his heart to leave immediately for the Isle of Harris in the Hebrides, off the northwestern coast of Scotland. He obeyed and left, even though he didn't know anyone in Harris. When he got off the boat and asked about the local church, he was directed to one of the elders. Three days before, praying in his barn, this elder had asked God to send Reverend Campbell. By faith the man had prepared accommodation for him and announced a meeting. Now he led Reverend Campbell to a house for a meal and then to the church, where a crowd had already gathered to hear him preach. Revival fell that night. But it would not have happened if Duncan Campbell had ignored the voice of the Lord. Obedience was essential.

This humble Scottish preacher deeply challenged me and the rest of our school to seek and obey God. Many of us, establishing ministries across Europe over the next couple of years, set aside one day a week to fast and pray for revival. We didn't do it to get something from God but to draw closer to Him. Fasting intensified intimacy and also taught us discipline. A couple of years later the Lord answered many people's prayers, including many desperate parents we had never met, by drawing many hippie kids into the Jesus Movement.

As our study tour was coming to an end, each of us asked God where He wanted us to go for the final two-month outreach. I got alone with God to pray about whether I was to go to French West Africa for my outreach. The thought came to my mind: *Not yet.* I was flooded by a sense of peace. The answer wasn't no; Africa was still in the future. As I continued to pray, the nation of France came to mind. Over the next few days, several others in the school received the same direction. Six of us formed the first French team I would lead together with Judi.

Back in Switzerland, two weeks before the outreach began, my team met for prayer. The Lord led us to pray Ezekiel 36 and 37 over France. Ezekiel 36 told of the Lord's promise to rebuild the ruined cities and multiply people, putting a new heart and spirit within them. Together we prayed, "Lord, please rebuild the spiritual foundations of France and multiply Christians within it." In Chapter 37 the Lord took the prophet Ezekiel into a valley of dry bones, telling him to prophesy three times over them. Life came into them, and they rose up a mighty army. "France is like a valley full of spiritually dry bones," we interceded. "We believe You want to bring life into it as the truth of Your Word is proclaimed. Lord, raise them up as a vast army as You bring revival."

A couple of days prior to departing for France, we gathered one final time to pray. Reona Peterson, a fellow SOE student, joined us in that meeting. I was ready to launch into intercession for France, but before I could, Reona began praying. She expressed awe and wonder at God's holiness. A fear of the Lord and hush of worship swept over us. With a sense of reverence, we asked God to show us what to pray for. In my mind's eye I saw the darkened outline of France with a heavy black cloud over it and immediately recognized it as Satan's oppression. Two arms came down from the cloud, holding the country firmly. I sensed the death grip the occult had on France. Sharing this with the team, I prayed, "Lord, show us how to pray."

God led us into spiritual warfare against the enemy. Calling for the Lord's angelic hosts to come do battle against this spirit, we cried out for the same fiery chariots that filled the hills around Elisha in 2 Kings 6:17. In the name of Jesus we bound the hands of the enemy and his forces that were gripping France. Pleading for mercy on this nation and freedom for its people, we prayed for salvation of the millions of lost souls in France. Then just as powerfully and forcefully as the prayers had begun, they ended. We sensed our prayers had come from the Holy Spirit, and I thanked God for opening our eyes to the invisible world over France. I began to realize that prayer was not informing God of something He was not aware of or trying to persuade a reluctant God to do something He didn't want to do. It was listening to Him to find out what was on His heart, and calling into being what God wanted to happen. As we "created with God," we were entering into the flow of history in this nation.

Some years later God showed me the importance not only of discernment in prayer but also of research in understanding how to minister to a nation's spiritual needs. While researching France's history, two of my French friends, Xavier Molinari and Isabelle Serex, learned of an event during the French Revolution that rocked the nation spiritually. On November 10, 1793, the people of Paris organized a Festival of Reason in Notre Dame Cathedral to replace Christian services with their own philosophy. They constructed a wooden Temple of Reason. An actress came out of the temple personifying the goddess of Reason, and received their homage and worship. The people sang a hymn: "Come, conquerors of the kings: Europe contemplates you; Come; upon the false gods extend your success; You, Holy Liberty, come inhabit this temple; Become the goddess of the French." This ceremony was repeated in other churches in Paris and in the provinces, dedicating all churches in France to the goddess of Reason. The idea that reason is supreme dominated people's thinking for centuries to come and closed people's minds and hearts to the gospel.

I realized that when sin enters a nation, it breaks down its spiritual walls of protection. Joy Dawson had quoted Ezekiel 22:30–31: "I looked for a man among them who would build up the wall and stand before me in the gap on behalf of the land so I would not have to destroy it, but I found none. So I will pour out my wrath on them and consume them with my fiery anger, bringing down on their own heads all they have done, declares the Sovereign LORD." God invites Christians to stand in that gap in the wall through prayer to hold back judgment and destruction. And this takes courage.

Much later I recalled the story in Numbers 13 and 14 of Moses sending twelve spies to explore the Promised Land. When the spies discovered giants there, ten of the twelve responded in fear and unbelief, and only two believed God could give them the land. Because of their disobedience, that generation of Israel wandered in the wilderness and never entered the Promised Land. Forty years later Joshua led the many battles it took to possess that country. Promises, I realized, are not automatically fulfilled. Instead, we must seize them by faith. Giants like Goliath (1 Samuel 17) and those in Canaan must be defeated; they don't just go away. The occult in France was like a giant. What we did in taking on this giant in our Promised Land would define our lives and ministry. Either we would run away defeated or we would be courageous and victorious with God's help.

On June 20 our team set out to France, our Promised Land, in an oversized VW bus, a former bread truck. Driving south we began witnessing in the campgrounds and beaches of southern France, where people from many European countries gathered to play. Judi and I discovered that French people were much more willing to talk about spiritual things while on vacation than they had been at their homes when we went door-to-door the previous summer in Paris and northern France. Their homes were their castles; you didn't approach uninvited. But their tents were accessible. In the campgrounds the people chattered with whoever tented near them.

That first evening, we drove our van into the beachfront town of Juan-les-Pins, fifteen miles from our campground. We brewed coffee on a camp stove inside the van and put up a sign that read "Discussion: Subject God." That night at our mobile coffee bar we witnessed to young people from Austria, France, Sweden, and the USA.

Around midnight I met a young man wearing a tee shirt, Levis, and sandals. With a gentle disposition, he asked what we were doing. I explained that we were discussing God. So he sat down on the edge of the curb and said, "Okay, let's discuss God." First, we got acquainted with each other. I learned his name was Samy, and he was from North Africa. Friendship was always a good starting point from which to share our faith. When I started talking about Jesus, he said, "Being brought up in a Muslim country, I believe God is one. If you can prove there is a Trinity, then I will listen to what you have to say." I could see in his steady stare that he was serious. *God, where should I begin?* I quickly prayed. I remembered our classes in Lausanne, and my thoughts cleared.

"The Law of God commanded death for the lawbreaker. For God to be just, He had to fulfill the just requirements of the Law. Law without consequences is only advice. If God would pardon us without penalty, then God's Laws would lose their power and there would be no justice."

Samy nodded his agreement. "I believe God is just," he said.

"But God brought justice and mercy together," I continued, "fulfilling our penalty for the broken law by substituting in our place the death of His Son, Jesus, on the cross. This enabled God to forgive us for breaking His law without us having to fulfill the consequence of death."

"But how can that be?" Samy asked.

After sending up another silent prayer to God for help, I responded, "God put a condition on receiving mercy: repentance—turning from our evil ways and turning to God." Then I discussed man's responsibility for his sins.

Samy asked, what if someone did this or that? At first he wouldn't acknowledge that he had done these things. A look of consternation marked his face. But soon he became transparent and began accepting the truth of what he was hearing. He began to see his responsibility for his sin and said, "I hear what you're saying, Joe." Yet he wouldn't yield his life to Jesus.

The next day we returned to Juan-les-Pins. Parking was almost impossible in this beach resort during the summer, and our modified van took two spaces. I prayed, "God would You open up a place for us as an indication of where to begin witnessing?" I drove back and forth along the beach for twenty minutes, looking for a parking place. Finding none, I drove out of town until I found an open space. As we unloaded our things, Samy walked by. We just "happened" to park right along his path. We walked together and spent the whole afternoon talking about Jesus.

Three days later, as I was driving the team to Juan-les-Pins, once again I asked the Lord to guide us to a parking place where we could witness. Soon after we parked, who should walk by but Samy. The team members smiled at each other knowingly, and I began talking with him. It would have been impossible to find him once he disappeared among the throngs of people on the beach. The Lord had set up yet another divine appointment.

Samy asked many questions about why people need a relationship with Jesus, and then he asked, "Now that I know about it and why people should have it, can you tell me how someone can receive it?" As I spoke about confessing and repenting of our sins, he clammed up. He remained defensive, not willing to admit he was involved in any wrongdoing, and the conversation ended. After that I had one more good discussion with Samy and gave him a booklet called *Conversion: True or False?*

Two days later, preparing to move on to another part of France, we went looking for Samy. We searched up and down the beach and at the café where he worked, without success. On July 11 our departure was saddened by the fact that we hadn't found him. He was so close to the kingdom.

Three weeks later, however, I received a letter from him forwarded via Lausanne. He had heard from those at his work that we had come looking for him. He spoke about the "splendid occasion" of his "encounter with God" and about the power of God he felt in his life helping him to do right and avoid wrong. He confessed the sins he had previously refused to acknowledge, and said that the pleasure he got from reading the Bible was stronger than any of his previous sins. He finished by saying, "The twentieth of July shall remain for me an unforgettable day, the turning point in my life."

Our whole team rejoiced at the victory God had won nine days after we had left, as God pursued this young man. We started to understand the significance of one soul to God. If our outreach to France had been only for Samy, it would have been worth it. We saw how far God would go to bring one person to Himself. We imagined the angels in heaven rejoicing with us.

At summer's end I closed out our team's finances. We had paid out $153 for engine repairs that were not in our budget, but we received unexpected gifts and offerings of $157. God had taken care of us. I now knew beyond a doubt that God's involvement with people was not just in Bible times but was real today. God had provided for us, directed us, and ministered through us.

All the teams returned to Lausanne for a reporting time the last week of August. The Stephenses and Boyds spoke about Germany, Al talked about Spain, and we covered France. With the school completed, Judi and I returned to California and reported to our friends and supporters the things we had seen God do. We began arranging our affairs so we could return full time to Europe.

While in San Jose I led our youth group in door-to-door witnessing in the neighborhood behind the church. As Judi and I rounded the corner of a street, I felt inexplicably drawn to the first house on a side street. We knocked. A young man answered and asked us who we were. He said, "My name is Steve. I'm a third-year political science student at San Jose State University." Within a short time we were talking about spiritual things. He remembered encountering a group of Jesus People playing guitars on the beach in Santa Cruz about a year before. "I was not at all interested in what they said, but then while I was hitchhiking about six months later, a person gave me a ride and talked to me about God." Steve said that when he left the car, the driver handed him the book *The Cross and the Switchblade* by David Wilkerson. "Now here you are at my door."

We talked at length, prodded by Steve's questions. He didn't give his heart to the Lord that day, but I gave him contact information for our youth group. A couple of months later he surrendered his life to Jesus. I thought of Jeremiah 29:13: "You will seek me and find me when you seek me with all your heart." Many people were not seeking God. My job was to stir a hunger in them to seek Him. If they did, they would find Him. Steve had said he was not interested in those Jesus People who were singing on the beach in Santa Cruz, but somehow they stirred a question or hunger in his heart. Then God led him to a Christian who gave him a book. Finally, Judi and I came to his door. The Lord was leading people across Steve's path to help him in his search for God.

This new understanding of Christian witnessing took a lot of pressure off me. I didn't need to be the one to lead someone to a profession of faith in Christ. My role was to discover where that person was in relationship with God and lead him or her at least one step further toward Him. If people were not seeking God, I needed to make them hungry for Him. If they were seeking Him, I needed to lead them further in that search. If they were well along in their search, I might have the privilege of leading them to surrender their life to Jesus. Getting to know people was the best starting point, and I loved seeing how God moved in each life. Missionary life, I learned, wasn't just about preaching sermons. It was telling people about Jesus. I could do that.

Yet I was left with one lingering question at the end of this period of ministry: what about the revival in France that God had led us to pray for?

Breathing Life into Dry Bones

IN EARLY 1971, just after my twenty-fourth birthday, Judi and I returned to Switzerland to begin YWAM French Ministries. The Stephenses and Boyds had moved to Germany, where they pioneered YWAM's ministry there. Al Akimoff had also left Switzerland and eventually moved to Holland, where, after working with Brother Andrew's ministry, he began YWAM's ministry into Eastern Europe and the former Soviet Union. A loneliness swept in, cold as the snow in the forest around us. I wondered if Judi and I would find new friends in this ministry we were pursuing.

I spoke to Loren Cunningham about establishing YWAM French Ministries that year and maybe beginning another ministry the following year. He smiled. "Joe, it takes three to five years to establish a business. That's also true for a ministry. It takes time to get to know the people and for them to get to know and trust you. You need to establish strong spiritual foundations for the work to survive once it's launched. Invest for the long term."

After that conversation, I put my next question into a prayer. "Lord, where am I to start this YWAM French ministry—here in Europe or in French West Africa?" I couldn't seem to get a clear answer.

While I wrestled with this question, I met several American missionaries who were in Switzerland studying French in preparation for going to West Africa. Like me, some found it difficult to master French. One of them told me, "I've been here a year and I'm still struggling. I want to get to West Africa, but as soon as I get there, I'll have to start studying the African trade language of my assigned region. I don't know how I'm going to do it." Since Europeans learned languages so much quicker than Americans, I wondered, wouldn't French-speaking young people make good missionaries to French West Africa? They would only jump from French to a local African language. This seemed easier than the two language jumps others had to make.

When it all came into focus, I sensed that God was not telling me what to do but was putting a choice before me. I felt Him assure me that I could go to Africa as a missionary, and He would bless me there. Or I could lay down my personal desires and mobilize a missionary army of young people who could evangelize all over Europe, French West Africa, and beyond. I could see the potential of this reservoir of European young people reaching many others. Together with Judi, I finally made my choice. I wasn't sure what impact my decision would have on my personal goal to go as a missionary to Africa, but I knew what I needed to do. *God, I want what will result in the most benefit to Your kingdom. I'm not sure what all it will mean, but I choose to stay in Europe to find and raise up that reservoir of French-speaking young people.* I didn't realize at the time how life-changing that decision would be.

Once the decision was made, Judi and I felt at peace again. We busied ourselves with praying and planning for an outreach to France the following summer. Once again Ezekiel 36 and 37 came into our prayers. We asked God to breathe His truth into France, to break up the spiritual dryness, and to raise up an army for His purposes out of the "valley of dry bones."

In July I led a team of nineteen young people to witness to troubled youth on the streets of Paris. We met every morning as a team for prayer and Bible study. In the afternoons and evenings we witnessed in the city. At that time Paris was part of the hippie trail. Youth traveled through Europe to Afghanistan and India, where illegal drugs were readily available. Many had dropped out of college to begin a search for truth; most tried to find it with the help of mind-altering drugs. One of the most successful evangelistic approaches to this group was that of teacher-scholar Francis Schaeffer, who began a ministry called L'Abri ("the Shelter") in Switzerland. In discussions with these young people, he would lead them to the logical conclusions of their beliefs—despair. Then he would quickly lead them to the understanding of who God is and why they needed Jesus. We adopted the same approach.

In early August, Reverend Clément Lecossec, founder of the Evangelical Movement among the Gypsies, held evangelistic meetings at a Gypsy gathering in Rouen, about seventy-five miles from Paris. Invited to help, we arrived amid dozens and dozens of horse-drawn carts and four-wheel-drive vehicles pulling caravans. The caravans covered an open field with a huge, beige tent in the center. Stout horses grazed in the field. The carts were colorful, but not as much as the people who sat around them cooking over open fires. The women wore long, multicolored skirts and shawls draped over their blouses. The men wore faded pants and shirts. This annual gathering brought together hundreds of clans of Roma people from all over Europe. Some lived in France, but many came from Central and Eastern Europe. The French called them *Tzigane*, a derogatory term. Many considered them stateless people, who roamed the roadways of Europe.

The meeting began with melancholy music from accordions, mandolins, violins, and guitars. The missionary preached about Jesus in the Romani language. When he invited people to turn from their sin and yield their lives to Jesus, many responded. Our team helped pray for them.

Someone pointed me to a man needing ministry. Without asking what he wanted (a mistake), I laid my hand on his shoulder and began to pray. When I said the name of Jesus, the man jerked forward. I felt a sensation like a growling bear rising out of this man, and at the same time I got punched in the stomach as the man's body convulsed. Staggering back, I opened my eyes. My gut ached as I sucked air.

After I caught my breath, I finally asked what the man wanted. He said, "Whenever I try to pray in that Name, I am convulsed and thrown to the ground. I want my freedom, but I can't get it myself."

"How did this begin?" I asked.

"My wife and I were missionaries in Borneo. She was bitten by a viper and died. I cursed God, saying, 'Satan is more powerful than God.' Returning to France, I became a spiritist medium and received supernatural abilities. I am serving evil, but I want to be free. Can you help me?"

I thought of Jesus' disciples who were unable to cast a demon out of a boy. Jesus told them, "This kind does not go out except by prayer and fasting" (Matthew 17:21 NKJV). I assured him, "We'll fast for the next two days, then return on Saturday to pray for you. Meet us here." He agreed.

I drove back to Paris and told the team about the man I had met, and several agreed to fast and pray with me. I sensed the Lord encouraging me: *Have not I spoken in My Word that I have given you authority to cast out demons?* I reminded the team of what Jesus said in Matthew 12:29: "How can anyone enter a strong man's house and carry off his possessions unless he first ties up the strong man? Then he can rob his house." I told them that as we fast we needed to ask God to bind the "strong man" who has taken possession of this man; then we could see him freed. I was so grateful that Joy Dawson had insisted we memorize a dozen scriptures of our authority over Satan. These would be very useful soon. I had learned them in both English and French.

On Saturday several of us returned to the Roma gathering. The missionary preached again, and when people responded, I looked for my friend. Sure enough, he came looking for me. I kept my eyes open as several of us prayed for him. When I spoke the name "Jesus," the man was thrown to the ground and began convulsing. A cloud of dust rose, putting a pungent smell of earth in the air. I prayed out, "It is written, 'I have given you authority to trample on snakes and scorpions and to overcome all the power of the enemy; nothing will harm you' (Luke 10:19)." A group of Roma pastors ran to join us. I prayed, "It is written, 'Submit yourselves, then, to God. Resist the devil, and he will flee from you' (James 4:7). I submit to God, I resist you in Jesus' name and you must flee." The man stopped thrashing, and his chest lifted off the ground like something left him. Then he began convulsing as another spirit battled to keep him.

I shouted, "It is written, 'And having disarmed the powers and authorities, he made a public spectacle of them, triumphing over them by the cross' (Colossians 2:15). You have been defeated by the cross. Be silent and flee in Jesus' name." Again he heaved upward. Then he began thrashing again. I continued, "It is written, 'You . . . have overcome them, because the one who is in you is greater than the one who is in the world' (1 John 4:4). Jesus in us is greater than you, forces of darkness. Be gone, in Jesus' name." He stopped and then he began convulsing again. I cried out, "It is written, Jesus said, 'On this rock I will build my church, and the gates of Hades will not overcome it. . . . Whatever you bind on earth will be bound in heaven, and whatever you loose on earth will be loosed in heaven' (Matthew 16:18–19). I bind you and send you to God's appointed place for you, not to return. In the name of Jesus, be gone."

This continued for ten to fifteen minutes. Finally, after one last battle the man stopped convulsing and lay still. I reached out my hand and helped him to his feet as he dusted himself off. We sat down, and he said, "I want to pray." He began a wonderful prayer, asking God to forgive him for what he had done. Then he said, "Jesus, I give you back my life. Please come in and fill my heart with Your presence." When he said, "Jesus," there was no reaction. He was free.

Then I prayed for him, asking Jesus to bless and restore to him the joy of his salvation. We embraced. I left him in the loving hands of a gracious God, who had delivered and forgiven him. The Gypsy pastors took over as we left.

As I drove back to Paris I prayed, "Lord, thank You for the deliverance You brought today. You are so powerful, loving, and forgiving. Please keep Your hand of blessing on this Gypsy man."

In talking with the youth on the streets of Paris, we discovered that many had dabbled in the occult. We saw the effects of this as we witnessed on the streets. Often we felt we were having a meaningful time of witnessing to people, but when we asked them if they wanted to invite Jesus into their lives, they would say no. We realized that the enemy was blocking them from responding to the gospel, so we took a different approach. When someone seemed open to the Lord, we would ask if we could pray for them. Many said yes. In our prayer of blessing upon them, we would quietly declare to the enemy that he was bound and couldn't hinder this person from understanding and making a choice for God. After saying, "Amen," we would ask them if they wanted to yield their life to Jesus. And more often than not, they said yes. Then, with their permission, we began the process of binding the enemy in their life and leading them to Jesus.

That summer I was intrigued by reports about a hippie commune in southern France near Nice. In mid-August we traveled there. Witnessing along the beaches, I listened for news of this commune. Someone told me it was in the mountain village of Coaraze, about fifteen and a half miles north. I drove with the team up a zigzagging mountain road to find this medieval village perched on a two-thousand-foot summit. At the center of the village sat a cobblestone square in front of a sunlit fourteenth-century church. Following an ancient narrow cobblestone street around the back of this square, we found the commune in an old abandoned stone building. They invited us in to a musty, windowless hall that looked like a former factory workshop. The entire left wall was covered by a mural with demonic shapes doing all sorts of unspeakable things. One of our team members, Denise, a sensitive Swiss art major, told me, "I can't look at that painting. If I do, I see it moving."

I talked with the leader and discovered this was a Satanist commune. He talked about the devil, and I talked about Jesus. Quickly he became very angry, so we departed.

The next morning at our campground we prayed for the commune and its leader. I said to the team, "This man is under demonic influence that has blinded his mind to the truth." From our experience in Rouen with the Gypsy man, we knew Jesus could deliver. So we took authority over the powers of darkness like Jesus told His disciples to do. We asked the Lord to give us an opportunity to witness to the commune leader when the enemy's lies had been silenced and he could understand the truth. I prayed, "We know he has the right to choose between Satan and You, Lord. We're not trying to take that freedom away. We just want him to have a window of time to understand and make a decision for or against truth."

That evening we returned to the commune. I tried to speak with the leader several times, but he was agitated. I asked God to give me that window when the man's spirit would be open to hear His voice. Around midnight he settled down, and finally I was able to begin witnessing to him. "You've told me about the people in your commune who have satanic power to do miracles. When Satan uses the supernatural, it is to lead people deeper and deeper into bondage. When Jesus performs a miracle, it is to help people, to set them free." I watched his eyes as I spoke. They were staring off into the distance just beyond me. Then he jerked his eyes back on me and said, "Excuse me. I was just reflecting on what you were saying." I thought, *Thank You for this moment, Lord, when his mind is not blinded and he is understanding truth.* We spoke for another fifteen minutes before he became agitated again, closing that window of openness. It was time to leave.

The next morning we met as a team to intercede for this man and his commune. I read from Matthew 12:43–45, "When an evil spirit comes out of a man, it goes through arid places seeking rest and does not find it. Then it says, 'I will return to the house I left.' When it arrives, it finds the house unoccupied, swept clean and put in order. Then it goes and takes with it seven other spirits more wicked than itself, and they go in and live there. And the final condition of that man is worse than the first." We prayed, "Lord, we realize this man has the right to choose for or against You. If he has chosen to come toward You and the truth, please arrange that he be home when we go there. If he has chosen against the truth, please arrange that he be gone. We don't want to produce a worse state in his life by trying to cast out what he doesn't want cast out. If he is there and willing, we believe You are able to deliver him, just like You did with the man in Rouen."

We fasted for the next three days according to Matthew 17:21 before going back up the mountain. On the third morning I read Ephesians 6:11–12: "Put on the full armor of God so that you can take your stand against the devil's schemes. For our struggle is not against flesh and blood, but against the rulers, against the authorities, against the powers of this dark world and against the spiritual forces of evil in the heavenly realms." Then in prayer I "put on the armor" listed in verses 14 through 20.

Instead of going with the whole team, I went with one team member named Tom to Coaraze. Judi dropped us off at the bus station in

Nice. The bus we took stopped at the square in front of the church. Walking down the stairs at the far side, we reached the commune. As we approached the building, we saw a van drive away. We knocked on the door and asked for the leader. The person answered, "He just left to Morocco for drugs and won't be back for a month." We had our answer: he had rejected the truth. So Tom and I ran to the square to catch the bus back.

The bus drove away right as we topped the stairs. Our running and shouting didn't stop it. We discovered it was the last bus for the day. We found no other options, so Tom and I hesitantly returned to the commune, explained our situation, and asked if we could spend the night. They agreed and showed us some floor space in a huge attic loft. I didn't get much sleep that night. Faces flying through the roof, apparitions, and hackle-raising sensations of an evil presence kept me up most of the night. It reminded me of the nightmares I had as a nine-year-old. I struggled through the night, resisting and binding the enemy each time something appeared. One phantom would depart, and I braced myself for the next onslaught. Tom had the same experience I had during the night.

I was never so happy to see morning arrive. We hurried to the square and sat in the sunshine, breathing sighs of relief as we waited for the bus. I was so glad I had not brought the whole team.

I learned much later that Coaraze had an ugly history of satanic influence. Legends of sorcery abound, including one that claims the devil was caught by the people of Coaraze and cut off his tail to escape. No wonder the commune found a comfortable home in that village.

Our time of ministering here brought mixed emotions. We rejoiced in the victories we saw when people wanted freedom from the occult. We were saddened when many others rejected it. Through those intense battles only a handful yielded to Jesus.

SEVEN

A Growing Vision

WHEN summer 1971 and the outreach in France ended, Judi and I returned to Lausanne, Switzerland. I helped staff a School of Evangelism for English speakers, and Judi took over responsibilities of the kitchen and food purchasing. That winter we also began preparations for the next summer's outreach in France.

As a new leader I would often go to Loren Cunningham, who was leading YWAM Lausanne, and ask him what he thought about various French ministry opportunities that surfaced. His immediate response was always, "What has God spoken to *your* heart about that?" As I shared the sense that stirred in my heart, he would affirm, "That sounds right. You're hearing from the Lord. Keep pursuing what your heart is telling you." In looking back at this season, I appreciated Loren's way of affirming my ability to hear from the Lord. This helped me overcome my insecurities as a young leader.

By this time two others had joined me and Judi to work full time in YWAM French Ministries, a Swiss woman named Ann Marie and a young American named Linda McGowen. Together the four of us prayed in earnest for France and the French people. Several times in March, as we asked God how to pray, He led us to pray for unity in the churches. A scripture stood out to us as we prayed, 2 Chronicles 7:14: "If my people, who are called by my name, will humble themselves and pray and seek my face and turn from their wicked ways, then will I hear from heaven and will forgive their sin and will heal their land." I wondered what seed of strategy was hidden in our prayer times.

One spring day a student from the English school came looking for me. She said, "I was just out in the forest praying for France. I saw a picture in my mind's eye. Is that weird?"

"I don't know," I replied. "What did you see?"

"I saw a picture of the map of France, brown, and looking like the surface of a garden where the soil had been prepared and seeds planted. As I watched, I saw two or three green shoots break through the surface and slowly begin to grow. Could that be from God?"

I smiled, remembering my team's experience in prayer before our outreach to France in 1970. "It could be. Two years ago, praying with a team, I also saw a picture in my mind. It looked like the shadowy outline of France, covered with a dark cloud. Two arms reached from the cloud and grasped the nation. We sensed God leading us to pray against the occult."

"So you think my prayer picture could mean something?" she asked.

"Yes," I said. "I think maybe God is telling us that He has heard our prayers over the past two years. I'm sure He has heard the prayers of many other Christians too. I think He's saying things have changed in France. What was once a hardened landscape of bondage is turning into a garden. Let's see if we can spot those two or three green shoots He is giving us this year."

Walking away with a skip in her step, the student smiled, having heard from her heavenly Father.

One day, just prior to the summer outreach, I got a phone call from Loren. He said a young Frenchman had come to his place and was interested in YWAM's summer ministry opportunities. I went over to meet him. He walked out and greeted me in English, introducing himself as Daniel Schaerer. When I asked him where he learned to speak English so well, he told me that he spent a year in the United States as a high school foreign exchange student. We stepped into my office and sat down in two straight-backed chairs. I asked Daniel to tell me more about himself.

"My father, a Swiss missionary, went to France to pastor a Protestant Reformed Church. He married my mother and began our family. I'm the seventh of eight children. I hadn't been following the Lord. Spiritually I had been practicing my parents' faith more than my own. Then I walked away from that faith, especially as I pursued my university studies in philosophy."

"So, how did you find the Lord and end up here in Lausanne?" I asked.

"My cousin is the leader of Hospital Christian Fellowship in France. She invited me to attend a conference they hosted in Austria two weeks ago. While I listened to the speakers and observed their lives, God touched my heart. Little by little I received what they were saying. Finally, I took a walk in a field nearby, cried out to God, and yielded my life to Jesus."

"That's great, Daniel."

"On my way home to tell my parents what happened to me, my cousin and I stopped through your center here in Lausanne," Daniel continued. "A young man told me about your summer outreaches. After going home and telling my parents about my newfound faith, I had a strong desire to return here to join in your summer ministry opportunities. So here I am."

I felt drawn to this young Frenchman and immediately invited him to join our team.

THAT summer we learned that Judi was pregnant with our first child. We took nineteen young people from seven countries to Bretagne (Brittany) in western France to work with a Swiss evangelist. Daniel Schaerer and Heinz Suter, a young Swiss, were our primary French speakers. Linda joined the team as well as Don Heckman, an enthusiastic tall blond American who had been in the Lausanne School of Evangelism.

We targeted Quimper, a city of sixty thousand inhabitants, where fishermen and merchant marines roamed the streets. Their wives wore tall lace hats, which to me looked like white, eighteen-inch stovepipes. We spent our mornings in prayer, our afternoons witnessing and prayer walking in town to discover God's heart for the people, and our evenings in evangelistic meetings.

I learned a key point that summer in praying for a nation. In a time of prayer God asked us to confess and ask forgiveness for France's sins, not in condemnation but in prophetic identification. He didn't do this, however, until we had enough love in our hearts for the country and its people to not become critical or negative. Reminded of Daniel's prayer of confession for Jerusalem in Daniel 9, I prayed, "Lord, forgive us, for we have sinned." I also recalled Leviticus 26:40–42: "But if they will confess their sins and the sins of their fathers . . . I will remember my covenant . . . and I will remember the land." As we confess for a people, I realized, God hears and he "remembers the land." This was our hope for France.

We opened a coffee bar in a small storefront where people came to talk about God. Across the street was an old movie theater. The manager, Yvon, was extremely resistant, and we prayed for him often. His wife discovered our coffee bar, and by the end of the summer she had yielded her heart to Jesus. Others also began responding to the Lord. By the time we left we had a group of fifteen to twenty people coming to the coffee bar regularly for fellowship and teaching. Roger, the Swiss evangelist who had invited us to come work with him, stayed there and pastored the group of new Christians. This church had developed unexpectedly; it was our first green shoot in that garden of France. My only regret was that Yvon hadn't given his heart to the Lord.

In September Judi and I and Daniel traveled to Munich, Germany, to participate in YWAM's 1972 Summer Olympic Games outreach. More than one thousand young people gathered there from all over the world. YWAM had expanded to countries all across Europe and Africa. We were separated and isolated in different places, and the Olympic outreach brought us all together for encouragement as well as ministry. Having been fighting battles against the Goliaths in our own promised lands, we all basked in the strength that came from uniting as one.

YWAM needed this time together just as much as the Munich Olympics needed our ministry.

During one of the training times inside a green-and-white striped circus tent, Loren challenged us with Nehemiah 4:19–20: "The work is extensive and spread out, and we are widely separated from each other along the wall. Wherever you hear the sound of the trumpet, join us there. Our God will fight for us!" Loren declared, "God wants us to come together in strength at times like this outreach. Let's agree that when one of our YWAM ministries has a need and sounds the trumpet for us to come, we'll respond. God may even ask you to sound the trumpet to rally us to your place of ministry." I wondered if this was something God had in His heart for France in the future.

A lifelong friendship began between Daniel and me that summer. When the outreach ended, he went to northeastern France to his first posting as a high school English teacher. He found one other Christian in the school where he taught, and they began meeting regularly for prayer. The prayer group slowly grew to about a dozen. Months later Daniel took over responsibility for a youth group at the Lutheran church in the area. It grew into over sixty young people following the Lord. I saw this as a second green shoot in France's garden.

At the end of the Summer Olympics outreach, Judi and I returned to Lausanne. With Judi's pregnancy, the multiplication in our family seemed to reflect what was happening with YWAM French Ministries. Both were developing.

God also was enlarging our vision during times of intercession. In a prayer meeting in November, He led us to pray for former French Indochina: Cambodia, Laos, and Vietnam. We prayed that He would spark a fire among Christians and raise up workers to minister there. Through this I realized that I needed to think bigger than just French Europe and French West Africa: I needed to pray for the whole French world, including the Pacific and Asia.

Near the end of the year I was scheduled to speak at a Sunday-morning worship service in Lausanne. I still struggled with a sense of inadequacy about preaching. This was now compounded by the fact that I had to preach in French. I knew I could lead teams and witness on the streets; I had taught in many team gatherings and had spoken and recruited in many church youth groups and evening meetings. But this would be my first time preaching in French at a Sunday morning worship service. The night before I was to speak, I slipped away to my room to pray.

"God, should I speak at the church, or should I get a French speaker from the team to do it?" I threw myself across the bed. "I need an answer from You."

Opening my Bible to my daily reading, I began reading Exodus 3 and 4. My heart started beating faster as I read. I saw myself in that passage, and I felt like God was speaking to me personally through it. In the story of Moses at the burning bush, I saw God calling a reluctant person to speak for Him to Israel and to Pharaoh.

Moses asked, "Who am I, that I should go?"

God answered, "I will be with you."

"What if they do not believe me?"

God assured Moses by giving him three signs to show them, one with his staff, one with his hand, and one with water from the Nile.

But Moses said, "O Lord, I have never been eloquent. I am slow of speech and tongue."

God responded, "Who gave man his mouth? Is it not I? Now go; I will help you speak."

"O Lord, please send someone else to do it," Moses begged.

Then it is recorded that God's anger burned against Moses. Finally, he said, "What about your brother, Aaron? I know he can speak well. He will speak to the people for you."

God challenged me with this story. Was I going to insist I was inadequate to speak, knowing God could help me? Or was I going to trust Him? I didn't want God to be angry or give me second best. I let out a deep sigh. "Okay, God, I choose to obey You and not settle for having an 'Aaron' speak for me. I believe You and will say what You ask me to say."

In fear and trembling the next morning, I preached on David's faith as he took on Goliath. It was hard to start as I faced my personal Goliath, but once I began, the fear lifted. It was easy because there was something I wanted to say. I challenged the people to see the French world as a Goliath that we needed to take on for the sake of the gospel.

Sure enough, they responded positively to the sermon. Several commented to me afterward how they had been encouraged. I sent up a silent prayer, *Thank you, Lord. You did come through. If You call me to speak Your Word and I say what You want me to say, You are able to help me get that message across.*

EIGHT

Mobilizing and Training French Speakers

IN JANUARY 1973 our first child, Lisa Lee, was born, arriving just before my twenty-sixth birthday. She had dark hair, brown eyes, and olive skin. It was exciting for Judi and me to be parents at last.

As our family was developing, so were my thoughts about YWAM French Ministries. I began sensing that God wanted me to "sound the trumpet," as Loren had challenged us in Munich from Nehemiah 4:19–20. With fear and trepidation I approached Loren about this. Once again he affirmed that I was hearing from the Lord and said I should pursue what was on my heart.

I invited all the YWAM ministries developing across Europe to come to Paris from July 1 to 14 and begin their various summer outreaches with a training and ministry time in France called *Revolution d'Amour* (Revolution of Love). Based on God's challenge to us through Ezekiel 37 to raise up a vast army, we began to recruit French and Swiss young people for the two-week Paris outreach. We also invited them to continue on afterward for the two-month summer ministry. Five new permanent team members joined me in recruiting, which gave us over ten people on our full-time team. Asking God to call French young people into full-time missions, we knew that would necessitate a training program for them. So we also began to recruit for our first French School of Evangelism in the fall.

As I prayed about the two-week Paris outreach, I asked God, the Lord of the Harvest, how many young people I should ask Him to send to us. I sensed in my heart the figure of two hundred fifty. Soon I was asked to do a live interview on the one French evangelical Christian radio station.

"You're planning to sponsor a summer outreach in Paris like the one last year at the Olympic Games," the radio interviewer prompted. "How many did you have in Germany?"

"Over one thousand," I responded with excitement.

"Will you have one thousand with you in France this summer?" he asked.

Letting myself get caught up in the thrill of the moment, I said without thinking, "Yes." As I reflected on this afterward, I was sorry for what I said, but I couldn't erase what people had heard.

During the preparations for this outreach I made frequent trips to Paris, meeting with as many pastors as I could. I also met a Christian businessman, Yves Cornaz, with whom I developed a close friendship.

As I looked for a space that would house several hundred young people, I had the idea of buying an old farmhouse outside Paris and using it as our first YWAM center in France afterward. We could house people inside the farmhouse and in tents in the surrounding fields. But no matter how hard I tried, I could not find a suitable place.

One day as I sat in my office preparing to make yet another trip to Paris, I said to the Lord, "Please give me understanding about our outreach housing. Is there a farmhouse in France that You have for us?" In my daily Scripture reading I read Proverbs 24:27, and my heart began to beat rapidly: "Finish your outdoor work and get your fields ready; after that, build your house." Could this be God's answer to me? Had I let myself get distracted by trying to find a permanent facility at the expense of doing the ministry, the outdoor work? "Lord, I trust You," I prayed. "I give you back this desire for our own place. Please lead us to Your housing provision for this outreach." I realized much later that if I had gotten a farmhouse then, I would have redirected my attention into fixing and maintaining it instead of developing the fledgling ministry emerging in France. God would have His perfect timing for the release of our first YWAM center there.

In mid-June, with two hundred fifty people enrolled for the Paris outreach, I knew I had blown it in the radio interview by responding to enthusiasm instead of God's word to me. I asked God for forgiveness and apologized to those working with me about declaring we would have one thousand participants. But I could see the damage had been done. When God sent over three hundred young people, instead of rejoicing at God's goodness, many were disappointed that we didn't have the one thousand. I learned a hard lesson: as leaders we can easily miss the mark regarding numbers and timing with our enthusiasm and vision.

On July 1 groups of young people came from all over Europe and North America to the campground we had reserved outside Paris in the village of Maisons-Laffitte. Sun-baked tents of all sizes housed the 330 people from twenty-four countries who had arrived overnight. They included seventy-six French and Swiss young people, for whom I was very grateful. We organized them into teams of twenty-five people, each having four cell groups of six members plus a team captain. Daniel, Don Heckman (who had been on our last outreach), and Heinz Suter (one of our new French Ministries team members) were among those leaders.

Each day half the group went into Paris to witness in several locations while the other half remained in camp for training and prayer. Then the next day, those who had remained went out to witness. Daily people responded to the Lord—every day one or two more than the day before. I heard a story about Tom, an actor with an American father and a French mother. He played a role in the Paris production of *Godspell*. Wondering what the Bible he quoted in his lines had to say about Jesus Christ, he began to read it. He found many contradictions between the attitude of the play and what he read in the Bible. In a state of confusion he met several young people from the outreach and found it easy to talk with them. They explained Jesus so simply. Tom realized that what the Bible said was true—that Jesus was the Son of God and he could receive Him into his heart. Without hesitation he prayed with the YWAM team members and gave his life to Jesus.

Another story I heard told of an elderly Parisian man who sat sunning himself in a park at noon one day. He observed our young people with faces so full of joy, talking excitedly as they handed out Christian literature. They came to the bench where he sat and handed him a gospel paper. When he saw it was the book of John, he thought of his wife, who had begun studying the Bible. He felt it had become a barrier between them. He wondered what motivated these young people to hand out those papers in the July heat. They shared with him how Jesus as a living Savior spoke to people through His word and wanted to speak to him as well. They said that following a religious system was not the same as knowing Jesus personally, and that he could get to know God through reading His message. The man came to realize that the Bible was not a barrier between him and his wife but actually a beautiful message they could share together. He promised as soon as he got home he would begin reading the Bible with his wife. The YWAMers wondered if she had been praying for this.

By the end of the outreach over eighty people had prayed in the streets to become Christians and agreed to receive a Bible correspondence course. We distributed approximately 250,000 copies of the Gospel of John in French, in newspaper form. At the end of the two weeks the other European teams returned to their countries of origin, and we continued with our own French outreach.

This was a summer of multiplication. Up until that year we had only one team ministering each summer. For the first time we exploded to six teams—four stationary ones and two mobile ones ministering in France, Switzerland, Belgium, and Holland—made up of fifty-four adults and three children. Some of the young people who had been working with me previously were now leading these teams. The Lord once again tripled our summer outreach participants and multiplied our teams. I began to see that trying to do more myself would only be "addition." But raising up and training young leaders made multiplication of teams and ministry possible. I could either try to protect the reputation of a group by doing more myself or take the risk of multiplying by raising up young leaders. I couldn't do both.

Judi and I, with six-month-old Lisa, visited each of the six teams. One team stayed in Paris to follow up with those who had responded to Christ. Heinz Suter led a team to Gagnières in central France. Don Heckman led a mobile team through France and Switzerland. Daniel Schaerer led a team to Quimper, ministering to the twenty-member church that resulted from the previous summer's work. They set up a coffee bar again and witnessed to many people. Linda joined the mobile music team, visiting and ministering with each of the other teams. A sixth team worked in a coffee bar in Biarritz on the Atlantic coast in southern France. Through that summer a growing group of missions-minded young people was developing.

Early that fall I attended a pastor's conference. Speaking with a missionary pastor from Paris, I asked him how things were going in that city. He responded, "I can't explain why, but for the first time in twenty years, I sense a lifting of the weight of oppression over Paris. Ministry is easier to do." I thanked the Lord that as our young people had prayed and witnessed that summer, God was working in that city.

On October 8, 1973, we launched our first YWAM School of Evangelism for French speakers with twenty-eight students. Heinz Suter worked as our French translator. The school followed a pattern of speakers and curriculum similar to the one I had gone through in English almost four years before. The positive response in the hearts of these French young people encouraged me. One student, a dark-haired, impeccable Parisian florist named André Sivager, caught my attention. Friendly and likeable, he was at ease talking with people. André often opened his heart to me and shared his spiritual struggles from the past. We spent many hours sharing and praying together as friends.

At the end of the three-month lecture phase, we decided not to organize a group outreach. Instead we arranged for students to go for three months to different YWAM centers or ministries. André led a group of five to Morocco to work with hippies and youth on drugs. Half the team stayed on permanently to work in Morocco at the end of the three months. André returned with the other half and joined our French Ministries staff with several other students.

I wrapped up the year personally by writing out nine short-term
and ten long-term goals for YWAM French Ministries. God was
expanding my heart to the whole French world, which includes nearly
fifty countries around the world that have historical and economical
ties with France, and where French is an official or trade language. The
short-term goals included recruiting 180 young people plus twenty
leaders for teams in 1974; preparing for the 1974 French SOE and outreach; incorporating YWAM in France; sending teams to Madagascar
and West Africa; preparing workers for the 1974 World Congress on
Evangelization, the 1974 Billy Graham crusade in Lausanne, and the
1975 Eurofest in Belgium; and moving our French Ministries offices
to new facilities. The long-term goals included mobilizing and training
one thousand French-speaking young people; establishing the French
SOE and outreach as an annual event at full capacity; establishing a
farm not far from the Lausanne center; finding additional housing next
to the Lausanne center; developing a center in Paris; opening a center
outside of Paris; establishing a farm in southern France; working in
France, Switzerland, and Belgium for evangelism and revival among
young people; expanding outreach to French Africa, French islands in
the Caribbean and the Pacific, and Asia; and mobilizing a large group
of French-speaking Europeans to the 1976 Olympics outreach in Montreal, Canada. I prayed God would fulfill these goals.

During the spring of 1974 we began preparations for the next summer outreaches. YWAM Holland organized a two-week training and
evangelism outreach in Amsterdam for all the YWAM teams in Europe,
similar to what we had done in Paris the previous year. Over 370
attended, including nearly one hundred French speakers from France,
Switzerland, and Belgium. After the two weeks in Amsterdam, I organized the French speakers into eight teams—one team to Belgium, one
to Switzerland, and six to France. Tom and Cynthia Bloomer, an American couple who just completed the English School of Evangelism, led
the team to Belgium. Tom was a tall, distinguished American with a
large handlebar mustache, who had learned French while serving in
Southeast Asia. Daniel Schaerer, back again for the summer, led a team
to Lorient in Brittany. André led a team to Switzerland, and Heinz took

a team to Dinard in France. Judi, Lisa, and I, traveling in a small green Fiat, visited each team over the course of the summer.

At the end of the summer all these teams converged at our center in Lausanne for two days of reporting what God had done. On the last evening I encouraged the young people to consider attending the next French School of Evangelism beginning in October. Daniel returned home to France, while Heinz, André, and the Bloomers stayed on to work as staff for the next French school. God always provided precious friends to work with and learn from as we pioneered new places. It seemed that a part of my calling was to invest in others as the work advanced.

And the work was advancing. During our spring, summer, and fall outreaches in 1974, seventeen teams ministered in French Europe with 177 total participants. We had tripled in size from the previous year. The Lord was beginning to raise up the army that he had promised and fulfill some of the goals I had set before Him the previous year.

He was also breathing new life into French-speaking Christians. With a heart to encourage the churches and society of the French world, we had launched YWAM French Publications in the fall of 1973. Having two new books ready to publish in French, we made arrangements with a printer in Paris to produce them. Facing a bill of $3,200 and no way to pay it, I asked the Lord if we should take out a loan. Two thoughts came to my mind: *Call Yves Cornaz*, my business friend in Paris, and *Read Proverbs 31:16*. First I got out my Bible and read, "She considers a field and buys it; out of her earnings she plants a vineyard." I sensed the Lord saying He would enable us to pay this bill, but the "earnings" from the book sales were to be like "planting a vineyard." We were to reinvest those funds in other books to launch the publication ministry. I promised the Lord I would do that.

Then I called Yves and arranged to meet him in Paris. Once there, I asked if he would go with me to meet with the printer, and he agreed. When we arrived, the printer told me, "Your books are ready to deliver. But you need to pay the bill first. Do you have the money with you?" As I stumbled over my words, trying to think of what to say, Yves pulled out his checkbook and asked the printer for the exact amount of the bill. Then he wrote a check, paying it in full. His gracious gift launched YWAM's French Publications.

In 1974 Linda McGowen produced our first French songbook, entitled *J'aime l'Eternel* (I Love the Lord). The songbook filled a need for praise and worship, and its popularity exploded across the French world. God's Spirit was touching French-speaking Christians, many of whom were now reaching out to their nation. I was thankful to the Lord for what He was doing in France.

NINE

Africa: Planning and Challenges

SPIRIT-LED pioneering begins with God. Acts 13:2 records the call of Barnabas and Saul: "The Holy Spirit said, 'Set apart for me Barnabas and Saul for the work to which I have called them.'" In the same way, the Lord set us apart for a special mission while I was planning our second French School of Evangelism in Lausanne in the fall of 1974. I tried to settle on what type of practical mission outreach we should do following the three-month lecture phase. Summer outreaches were easy to organize using vans, tents, and camp stoves, but this outreach would begin in late December when snow covered the ground.

Loren Cunningham, who had moved to Hawaii, came through Lausanne, and I told him about our first school and the challenges with this next one. Loren asked, "Have you considered doing an outreach with the whole school together in one group?"

"Well, no," I admitted, "I don't know how we can do that. The lecture phase ends in late December, and winter is a terrible time to camp. It would be impossible to sleep in tents."

"That's true, Joe," Loren replied, "but have you ever considered driving down to Africa for your outreach? In several days you would drive off the continent of Europe and be in warmer weather. Camping would be possible. You would have an amazing time of ministry."

As Loren spoke, something inside me leapt with excitement. Could God be opening a doorway into Africa? "That sounds terrific, Loren. Let me pray about it."

After this conversation I took a long look at a map of Europe and Africa. We had always done our outreaches by road to keep costs down. Driving also afforded us the advantage of having our own transportation and housing once we reached our destination, especially when we knew no one there. The only routes overland to French West Africa passed through the Sahara Desert. I was excited about the possibility of ministering in Africa, but I was also concerned about the challenge of driving through that wasteland. The Sahara is nearly the size of the continental United States, the biggest desert in the world. It covers more than one-third the continent of Africa. People spoke of distances in days of travel, not just in miles. Was this a human idea, or was it a God-inspired vision? I needed to hear from the Lord.

The more I prayed, the more I felt it was something God wanted us to do. But I needed to be sure. Just prior to the beginning of the school, I asked the Lord again if He would confirm the outreach we were considering. I had the impression, *Read Isaiah 43–45.* My heart quickened as I read Isaiah 43:19: "See, I am doing a new thing! Now it springs up; do you not perceive it? *I am making a way in the desert* and streams in the wasteland." Upon reading this, I knew this outreach was no longer my vision but God's. This passage also confirmed to my heart that it was right to go overland through the desert to West Africa.

The following week a Christian leader advised me not to take the students across the Sahara. "That trip is too dangerous and risks lives needlessly." I thanked him for his concern, but the passage in Isaiah 43:19 continued to encourage me. Even if it was dangerous, God was able to take care of us. If God said He would make a way in the desert, then I needed to trust Him. Doing new and risky things requires absolute trust in God and in what He has spoken. Radical obedience opens doors for God to work in and through us.

On October 2 we started the school with another twenty-eight French-speaking young people from France, Switzerland, Canada, Britain, and Sicily.

Having received God's word about His "making a way in the desert," I needed to begin the hard work of putting this word into action. I talked with people who had driven through the Sahara. I purchased a book from the Swiss Touring Club that gave a mile-by-mile description of the three roads that crossed the desert. I calculated the longest distances between the oases where water and gasoline were available, the amount of fuel a Volkswagen van would consume over sand, and the amount of water each person would drink daily. That way I could figure how much total weight we needed to carry for twenty people and thereby figure how many vehicles we needed. My conclusion: four vans carrying five people each could handle the extra weight of all the water, food, tools, gasoline, suitcases, tents, and camping equipment, and still be able to drive over sand.

While on the phone ordering four old VW vans for purchase from a mission in Holland, I recalled the composition I had written when I was in the fourth grade. My arms tingled with goose bumps. *I have already fulfilled much of that by coming to Europe and learning French*, I thought. Now I was embarking on the last part of what I had written—driving down to West Africa as a missionary. God was fulfilling His word in my life. I wondered what significance this trip would have on my future ministry.

After obtaining the vans, I arranged for the mechanic at our YWAM transportation center in Germany to recondition them for the Sahara. He installed truck oil-bath air filters, fitting them with a special air scoop above the roofline. He rebuilt the suspension and added auxiliary oil radiators to increase the oil to cool the engines. Finally, he put rugged tires on all the vans.

The Swiss Touring Club book gave specific lists of equipment needed for desert crossings. I began purchasing gasoline jerry cans, army shovels, tools, spare VW parts, camping and cooking equipment, water containers, water filters, and a medical kit. We had two sand ladders made for each vehicle. These 3/8-inch black-pipe ladders were ten inches wide and six feet long. They would be put under the wheels of a vehicle when it got stuck in the sand so it could drive over them to gain speed before encountering the sand again.

As the lecture phase closed, several students dropped out. There would be nineteen of us going, sixteen students and three staff—André Sivager, Marie Christine Wasem, and me. Judi would not be going with us, because she was pregnant with our second child and not in a condition for crossing the Sahara. She would stay home to take care of little Lisa.

Eight people in our group were assigned as drivers, two per vehicle. One of our students, Gérard, was a trained mechanic. One student, Evelyne, was assigned responsibility for our food; another for our water supply; another for our finances; another for keeping our daily log. Three were nurses to be on call as needed. We planned like it all depended on us, but prayed like it all depended on God.

Two other YWAM schools heard about our trip and asked to join us. Two nights before we departed, Keith and Marion Warrington came down to Switzerland in three VW vans with seventeen people from a German school. Don and Evey Heckman from a British school would join us en route, with eight people in a Ford Bedford. Once we met in southern France, we would make a caravan of forty-four people in eight vehicles. After crossing the Sahara, the German school would go to Nigeria, the British school to Ghana, and our school to Burkina Faso, Ivory Coast, Mali, and Senegal.

Wearing my overcoat, hat, and scarf on that rainy, cold day of December 28, 1974, three weeks before my twenty-eighth birthday, we prepared to depart from Lausanne. The driveway at our training center looked like a mushroom patch of tents in every stage of assembly. Testing these now would help prevent disappointment later. People worked in a beehive of activities, loading each van with nine jerry cans, cooking equipment, food, water filters, water containers, small suitcases, and personal belongings. The tents were re-bagged and loaded onto the luggage racks.

Before leaving we gathered in a circle, held hands, and prayed. "Lord, please watch over us on the road. Keep us safe and fulfill all the purposes You have for us in Africa. Also, please watch over our families staying here. We ask this in Jesus' name. Amen." I kissed Judi good-bye and then got down on one knee, hugging our two-year-old daughter. "Lisa, you know this trip through the Sahara is no place for you and Mommy. Mommy is expecting another baby. Please take care of her for me." Lisa nodded as she squeezed my neck.

Saying our good-byes in the driveway, I could not have imagined the adventures, challenges, and dangers that awaited us, and how God would see us through. Over the coming months I would continually be brought back to His promise in Isaiah 43:19—He would make a way in the desert.

We began our journey heading south through snowy mountain passes. Five miles from our destination that first night, we got a flat tire. We broke our wrench, unable to loosen the over-tightened lug nuts. The next day in an auto shop, a mechanic removed and greased all our lug nuts. In repairing the flat we discovered that we only had ten patches, so we purchased at least fifty more, plus extra wrenches. I thanked the Lord for His faithfulness in allowing that flat tire to happen while we still had the availability of garages and wrenches. My stomach knotted as I thought about what could have happened if we hadn't discovered this problem until we were in the middle of the Sahara.

The British school joined us in southern France. Traveling through Spain, we crossed the Straits of Gibraltar on a ferry. On January 3 we reached Africa at Ceuta, Spanish North Africa, and then entered Morocco. In Tangiers I learned that the German and British schools still needed to get Algerian visas, which our team already had. So they left for the embassy in Rabat, and our school camped in Fez, a town on the road to Algeria. As temperatures dropped below freezing that first night, some students murmured bitterly about the delay to get visas and the uncomfortable living conditions. "We obtained all our visas before leaving Switzerland, so why haven't the other teams?" they complained.

Though the question they raised was understandable, the dissension weighed heavily on me as I lay shivering in my tent that night. I remembered the story of the children of Israel wandering for forty years through the desert. Numbers 21:4–5 says, "The people grew impatient on the way; they spoke against God and against Moses." As a result, "The LORD sent venomous snakes among them" (21:6). *I need to speak to these students,* I thought. *They can choose to adjust their heart atti-tudes. If this trip is too difficult for them, they can return home from here. But once we leave here, we cross the point of no return, and they will have to make it through the desert.*

So the next day, with another staff member, I met with each of these students individually. "We may encounter many more difficulties along the way," I said. "But murmuring and complaining won't help anyone. Ask God to help you cope with these circumstances."

A couple of them put their fears into words. "What if I can't cope with the conditions?"

"If you think the conditions will be too hard for you," I responded, "you can return home from here. We can drive you to the port, put you on the ferry, and in Europe you can take the train home. But once we start south, that will no longer be possible."

We prayed with students and asked each of them to take time to consider what they should do. Soon afterward each student returned to me with an apology for murmuring, a changed heart attitude, and a desire to continue through the desert. We accepted their apologies and prayed for God to help them.

Meanwhile, the other students had gone into town that day to buy warm blankets, since nighttime temperatures dropped below freez-ing. Several guys bought *djellabas*, traditional hooded, long-sleeved, floor-length robes worn by Moroccan men, made of thick wool that looked like blanket material. I could see the usefulness of the djellabas in cooler weather, but I wondered what use they would have once we headed south and encountered warmer weather. To me the djellabas seemed like excess material to carry in our already overcrowded vans.

When the German and British schools returned from Rabat, we learned that all but five Germans in Keith's school got their Algerian visas. Spending Friday, January 9, in the campground at Fez, we prayed in small groups for the needed visa and for the ministry in West Africa. The next day the German school returned to Rabat to make one final attempt to obtain visas, and our British and Swiss schools drove ahead to the oasis town of Ghardaia in north-central Algeria. Ghardaia was on the paved road leading south into the Sahara. There we could make final preparations for the desert crossing. With no means of telephoning each other, we would find a campground and wait there until the German school showed up.

Arriving around midnight in Ghardaia after a fourteen-hour drive, we found a campground on the edge of town, surrounded by a high fence. After much knocking, someone grudgingly admitted us and told us to be quiet as we pitched our tents in a grove of date palms. But this place proved to be anything but quiet. Before sunrise the next morning, a loud, wailing cry woke me up. Just across the road a mosque, with its minaret, boomed its first of five daily prayer calls.

After breakfast I drove into Ghardaia along a palm-lined road and was surprised to discover it to be a city of around ninety-thousand inhabitants, situated at the edge of the *petit* (little) Sahara. At the center of the old town, built on a slight hill, was a honeycomb of white, box-shaped houses connected via courtyards. I learned that the white paint and designs on the houses indicated the owners had made a pilgrimage to Mecca. Sprawling down from the cluster of houses was the market and commercial district where I was able to find lantern parts we needed.

Back at the campground our students prepared materials, replenished our food supply, and refilled propane tanks. In doing these chores the students met and shared their faith with local shopkeepers and other campers. We met a former Red Cross worker who had been through the Sahara seventeen times. He said, "I've done many things with North Africans, but I have never been invited into one of their homes. If you ever get invited in, please tell me what it's like." I wondered if we ever would.

By Friday, nearly a week since we had left the German school in Morocco, we had completed our preparations and were ready to go. I noticed a small group of students in animated discussion and began to pick up a quiet but bitter murmuring again in our ranks.

That morning, as the students met for prayer, the German group arrived, sparking much joy. Keith explained that the five Germans were refused Algerian visas, so he sent them with a staff member and one of their vans by ship to Dakar, Senegal. From there they would drive to

Nigeria, arriving about the same time as those going through the desert. This meant we would now be thirty-nine people traveling in a convoy of seven vehicles.

The following morning, on my twenty-eighth birthday, all the tents were taken down and the vehicles packed. The vans lined up at the gate, ready to depart, when one of the German vehicles suddenly lost all its motor oil. Unable to find the cause of the leak, we towed the van to a garage in town. The rest of us parked and waited. News came that the motor had to be removed for repairs.

The wind began blowing that afternoon, and sand flew everywhere. Since the motor was in pieces at the garage in town that evening, we prepared to spend the night at the campground again. We couldn't set up the tents because of the strong wind. The girls slept in the vehicles, and the guys slept in some old bamboo huts. That night the wind blew off most of the thatched roofs, and it began to drizzle. Some found plastic to cover their huts, while others of us just hunkered down into our sleeping bags to wait it out. In the morning the wind blew even more fiercely. Grabbing my sleeping bag, I ran and squeezed into my own van. Most had not slept well that night.

While I sat in the van hoping the storm would die down and hoping for news of the German van, I heard two of the five daily prayer calls from the mosque across the street. Though it was late morning, I could no longer see the sun. From the sound of wind and blowing particles, I imagined the sandstorm stretched to the horizon. I could hardly see outside. To keep the paint on our vans from eroding away and the glass from being blasted permanently opaque by the sand, we rubbed grease on the front of our vans and the windows.

Back in my vehicle I saw a blur wrapped in a dark djellaba scurry from the camp office to open the gate. The gate whipped open in the wind, pulling the person with it. One of our vehicles drove through and parked. I pushed my door hard against the wind, jumped out, closed the door, and headed to the newly arrived vehicle. As I pressed against the storm, sand stung my face, blew into my mouth, and gritted on my teeth.

"What's the situation with the van?" I asked.

The driver explained, "We can't find the parts we need in Ghardaia. The garage owner gave us the name of a Volkswagen mechanic in a village one hundred miles east of here. He might have the parts."

Keith went with the driver to the telephone exchange in town to call the mechanic, while Don and I ran to the camp office. We asked the camp manager if we could get to the next oasis town, El Golea, 152 miles south, in this storm.

He explained, "Though the road is paved, drifts of sand blown from the storm will soon block it. After the storm, it will take road crews about three days to clear the way again. If you don't leave soon, you will have to wait here several more days."

Don and I ran back to my van. When I pulled the door open, voices from inside gasped from the invasion of sand. Inside the van our feet scraped on the sand-covered floor. Lidia Guidice, our one teammate from Sicily, popped her round, smiling face up from the seat behind me and asked, "What's happening, Joe?"

"We don't have the parts yet," I said. She sat back, looking disappointed. Remembering a Sicilian expression I learned as a child from my grandmother, I attempted to say, "Just be patient."

Laughing, Lidia blurted out, "That was a good try, but you still can't speak Italian."

When Keith returned a couple hours later without any parts, my stomach knotted. Once again I picked up rumblings of impatience from some of the team. *These last couple of days of delay have not been easy for them,* I thought.

I tried to communicate with the team as much as possible to keep everyone informed of our situation, but there wasn't much to share. Waiting was difficult. With the wind blowing so hard, we still couldn't pitch tents. It had been over four hours since the camp manager told us we had to leave soon if we wanted to make it through to El Golea. I wondered if the road was already impassable.

Keith, Don, and I prayed, asking the Lord what to do. We sensed that Don and I were to leave with the British and Swiss schools. Keith would remain with the German school until their vehicle was repaired. Though we didn't fully understand why, we sensed that God had His purposes in this. Being pressed to leave in a sandstorm, I didn't give much thought to what those purposes might be. All I knew was that by faith we were to go. I knew God would see us through. But in my heart I was asking, *Lord, where are you in all these delays? What's happening?*

TEN

God's Delays

THE desert wind howled with new fury as our little caravan drove out of Ghardaia at 5:45 PM. It nearly blew off the campground gate as our German team struggled to hold it open as we drove through. The storm stirred up so much dust that it seemed like we were driving into a brown blizzard. I drove the lead vehicle, switching on my headlights as we pulled onto the road. But with so much sand in the air, the lights seemed useless. I turned them off and slowed.

At the outskirts of town we encountered our first drift. I swung to the edge and sailed over the small shoulder at its base. The students usually chatted as we drove along, but now they rode in silence. I didn't know whether they were still tense from waiting so long in Ghardaia or whether it was the frightening travel conditions. *Maybe they're just praying we get through this awful sandstorm,* I thought.

Farther along, a drift eighteen inches high and twenty feet wide blocked the entire road. When I saw it, I could feel my heart quicken. I thought I could get over it if I avoided the center, so I veered right and floored the accelerator. The tires spun wildly as they hit the sand. The van slowed slightly, but having gained enough momentum, it pushed through. Looking in my rearview mirror, I watched the other vehicles pass over the drift where my van had cut a path. I could still hear my heart beating in my ears as I gulped a deep breath and kept on driving.

We crept along mile by mile through similar drifts, following the same procedure. We had not encountered full-blown sand dunes, but at one point, while squinting into the blur of flying sand, I heard Lidia shout, "Joe, watch out for that sand—it's blocking the whole road!" I swerved, hitting the accelerator. We bounced off our seats as the van sailed and spun over the drift. A few bags went airborne, but no one was hurt. I then realized that darkness was falling. No wonder I hadn't seen that drift. I turned on our lights again.

A while later one of the vans got stuck in the sand. I stopped my van and got out to go push the stuck van. The strain sent my adrenalin racing. Every moment outside in the stinging sand made me desperate to take cover. When I finally got back inside my van and continued driving, it felt eerily quiet. Time seemed to slow down. I stared at my odometer, which showed we had hardly traveled any distance since the last time I checked. The muscles in my neck and shoulders were tensed like knotted rope. I knew we would meet no other vehicles on this road until the storm ended and road crews cleared it. If we got totally stuck, we would be stranded with no one to help. I had to be careful every mile of the way. By 1:00 AM, seven hours after leaving Ghardaia, I was battling not only the wind and sand but also exhaustion. The farther I drove, the heavier my eyelids felt.

"Watch out, Joe!" someone suddenly shouted. My eyes snapped open and focused on a huge drift we were approaching at too high a speed. I slammed on the brakes and the van skidded to a stop just before we hit the enormous dune.

"How can we get through?" Lidia asked, with a tinge of fear in her voice.

"I don't know. The sand is spread out for a long way in front of and behind it."

"We can shovel a way around it," suggested one of the guys.

"Let's try it," I said. "Some of you grab shovels and come with me."

The dune was so high that the only way to pass was to skirt around it. Several of us shoveled furiously, leveling the side of it just enough for a vehicle to pass over. Then, backing my van up, I took a running start, flooring the accelerator. The van lurched as it struggled through the dune. Some people ran alongside, pushing. Then, to my horror, the van hung up in the sand. Without prodding, other students jumped out and started shoveling again and dug away the sand in front of and underneath the van. Then, with people pushing, I revved the engine and let out the clutch. Wheels spun as we slowly moved forward. When the wheels reached the pavement, a huge cheer rang out. I slowed, pulled out of the way, and helped the other vehicles get over the dune. We continued our trek to El Golea.

At 2:00 AM, after eight hours and 152 miles, we arrived safe but exhausted. We had gotten stuck six times, and six times found a way through. Too tired to look for a campground, we parked in a field with several big sand drifts to our left. We slept sitting in our vehicles for the small remainder of the night.

By morning the wind had died down. The sand drifts that had been to our left several hours earlier had been blown to our right. After breakfast we went into the oasis to find a place to stay while we waited for the German team to catch up. The campground had closed months before, but a man from the tourist office arranged for us to be housed in an empty school building. As a goodwill gesture he gave each of us a "desert rose" dug from the area, a small round rock with protrusions that resembled an opened flower.

The next day we picnicked on a nearby mountain. From the top we gazed at a stark desert landscape stretching out as far as the eye could see. It contrasted with a dark green circle of palm trees (almost two hundred thousand, I was told) that made up the oasis town of El Golea. There was no gradual fading from greenery to desert: where there was water, there were palm trees; where the water ended, the trees ended.

As we rested in the school building that afternoon, we heard shouting and a sharp knock on the door. Outside stood a distraught Algerian man saying in French, "Do you have a nurse? I have an emergency! I need help!" Someone ran and got Evey Heckman. "Does anyone have type AB positive blood?" he pleaded. "My sister gave birth in the clinic and has started to hemorrhage. The clinic doesn't have this type, nor does anyone in town. I heard there was a group staying at the school, so I came here to ask." Evey's husband, Don, had that rare blood type, so he went to the clinic and gave blood.

The next day the brother who had come to the school invited Don and Evey to his house for couscous. On the way, Don and Evey went to the clinic, where Don gave blood again, and visited the woman and her infant son.

Meanwhile, someone located a Turkish bath with scheduled hours for men and for women and children. Several of us guys went during the men's hours. After undressing in an outer room, we entered a tiled room. In the middle, dense with steam, sat a raised basin and fountain flowing with hot water. The walls were filthy with mold, but since I hadn't had a bath in sixteen days, I overlooked it. Sitting on low wooden stools, we joyfully washed and then scooped water in a small bowl and splashed it over us, rinsing off the soap. It felt unbelievably good. When the hours for women and children came, several of our young women refused to bathe because of the filth and a fear of fleas and lice. This was a great disappointment for them and added to the tension some felt.

The man whose sister needed the blood transfusion invited our whole group to his home that evening for tea. When we entered his house, his wife greeted us without the customary veil. She was a lovely woman with a gentle smile. He explained that Muslim women must always wear a veil when outside the home, but never inside. I remembered the Swiss camper in Ghardaia who, after seventeen trips through the Sahara, had never been invited into a Muslim home. *That must be the reason strangers are not often invited in*, I thought. So I asked our host about it.

With a smile he looked at Don. "That's true, but you're not strangers. This man's blood now flows in our family."

We were escorted into a room with large cushions for seating. We sat leaning against walls covered with beautiful tapestries and oriental rugs. One tapestry showed three colorful, turbaned horsemen with spears fighting two lions among palm trees in an oasis. It was a festive evening with delicious honey-coated pastries and the traditional three cups of strong, very sweet mint tea. The man and his wife explained some of their customs, inviting Evey to try on the woman's wedding dress and veil. Her husband taught several of us how to tie on the traditional *shesh*, a brown muslin turban worn by men for protection in the desert. Then some of us told our hosts about customs and ways of our nations and what we believed as Christians.

Late at night we returned to the school, excited about the evening we had just spent with this family. I thanked the Lord for opening the home of that precious Algerian family to us on our very first trip through the desert. I marveled at how He had arranged whatever was needed to accomplish His purposes—even AB positive blood! *I hope my team is beginning to see the beauty of the people around us and the purposes for why God sent us on this trip*, I thought, beginning to relax. *Maybe the tensions are over.*

At half past midnight I heard the gentle rumblings of a VW exhaust system. Running outside, we greeted the German team with hugs of pure joy as they arrived from Ghardaia.

In the morning we told Keith and his team about our experiences in El Golea.

"Wait till you hear how God provided the parts we needed in Ghardaia!" Keith exclaimed. "We gave up our search and were about to leave for the port in Algiers when two Europeans, coming up from the Sahara, drove into the campground. Hearing our dilemma, they reached into their supplies and pulled out the needed parts. Since they didn't need the parts anymore, they gave them to us."

God took care of all of us—Keith in Ghardaia and the people He wanted us to reach in El Golea. If Keith's vehicle hadn't broken down in Ghardaia, and if the British and Swiss schools hadn't departed for El Golea in the midst of the sandstorm, we would never have met the Algerian family. *Thank you, Lord, for arranging these delays*, I prayed. *Help us to see the people You want us to minister to every time we have an unexpected delay. And feel free to stop us anytime You want us to minister to someone.*

Late that morning we departed for the oasis of In Salah, 250 miles south. On the last stretch of paved road we would encounter for weeks, we met only one vehicle during the seven-hour drive. Both of us slowed, each moving half off the single paved lane in order to pass.

We spent the night in In Salah and early the next morning prepared for our entry into the *grand* Sahara. Don Heckman and I each bought a *shesh*, the ten-foot lengths of muslin cloth we had learned about in El Golea. They would protect us from the heat and sand.

At the police station we registered our proposed itinerary, projecting an arrival time in three days at our next destination, the oasis town of Tamanrasset. This was radioed ahead to Tamanrasset's police station. We were to immediately register there once we arrived. If we didn't show up within a reasonable period of time, they would send a search party for us. We also sent a telex message to the school in Lausanne, giving them our travel plans.

In this next phase of the trek we would leave the desert floor and climb into the rugged Ahaggar Mountains. We filled jerry cans in each vehicle with enough gas and water to make the 430-mile trip. There were no reliable water sources or gas stations in between. Because of the rough terrain, we expected the engines would use one and a half times their normal consumption.

Just out of El Golea we left the paved road and entered a wide, dusty, desolate washboard track. A huge cloud of dust approached us from the horizon. We stopped and stared in amazement, trying to figure out what it was. As it got closer, we could see a ten-wheel cargo truck. As the dust engulfed us, the truck stopped and the driver reported the road conditions. This was part of the unwritten law of the desert: you always stopped when meeting someone, either to exchange news or to offer help; conditions changed very rapidly out there. We thanked the driver and drove on.

At the first stretch of unmarred sand dunes, we stopped. Everyone got out and ran up the dunes, giggling like children on a playground. Reaching the top of a dune, we rolled down it gleefully. That playful incident seemed to release the tension from our many days on the road. Regaining our composure, we were ready to move on.

During this first stage of our crossing, we saw varied terrain. Moving up from the desert floor, we scaled rocky, barren hills and climbed onto a massive plateau. The lonely desolation was beautiful. Small piles of stones every few yards marked the weather-pitted road. Most of the way the track was visible, but as terrain changed, we had to be careful not to lose our way.

I learned to write Judi on aerograms as we drove on these rough roads. I wrote quickly as our vehicle bounced up in the air and stopped writing before we thudded at the bottom. Sometimes a word took several bumps to complete. I mailed them at the post in the next oasis.

At sundown we made camp, always a fun time of day. Team members gratefully stumbled out of the stuffy vans. We arranged the vehicles in a wide circle, refueled, and built a fire in the center of our camp with firewood we had gathered in an oasis town. There was no firewood in the desert. The back of one van opened up into our kitchen, where Evelyne prepared our one hot meal of the day. Everyone else pitched tents. With the work done and the meal prepared, we sat around the fire to eat and sing. Those evenings impacted us all, as we sang our worship to God under a spectacular star-filled sky that stretched from horizon to horizon. All our tension and fatigue melted away as we watched falling stars streak across the sky. Time for sleep came all too quickly.

At 4:00 AM we got up and took down the tents. After eating Cream of Wheat, we each got a soup bowl of water to wash ourselves. With a little ingenuity we could wash quite well with this small amount of water. Then we packed everything away for another day on the road.

As soon as the sun peeked its golden yellow glow over the edge of the horizon, we continued on. Soft, wind-sculpted sand surrounded us as far as we could see. While everyone focused on getting through the physical challenges of the desert, the emotional tensions seemed to disappear. The first hour of travel was set aside for personal devotions, and it was not hard to see and feel God's presence in the stark beauty of this place. It was a relief for me to be concentrating on road conditions instead of team struggles.

The next morning, off to the left of the track I saw a herd of more than twenty camels slowly moving away from us. As we stopped to watch them, a Tuareg nomad on camelback approached, wearing a long muslin cloth wrapped many times around his head and several times around his mouth and nose. I learned later that Tuaregs are the only Muslim group whose women do not veil their faces; the men do. As we were unable to communicate with him, he soon rode off.

Just before midnight on the third day, we arrived in Tamanrasset and found a place to camp. First thing the next morning we handled all our formalities at the police station. Finding a five-star hotel with a telex machine, we sent a message to Lausanne announcing our safe arrival. Then it was time to get clean. The Turkish bath was closed, but they agreed to open specially for our group. To the relief of many, it was much cleaner than the one in El Golea. Getting clean boosted everyone's morale. That night we had a special chicken and rice dinner, followed by a time of worship before bed. Everyone was thanking the Lord for His safekeeping of us thus far.

When we woke up, we began preparing in earnest for the longest stage of our desert crossing. This 557-mile stretch of sand would take at least six days to cross. Each vehicle had to carry a maximum load of fuel and water. Since vehicles driven over sand use twice their normal consumption, each van carried nearly half a ton of liquid in jerry cans. We had to maintain a delicate balance. Too much fuel and water meant our vehicles would bog down, and spinning wheels struggling out of sand used up even more fuel. But if we didn't carry enough, we risked not reaching our destination.

The next morning we departed. This time we not only had to file our proposed itinerary and timing with the police, but we also had to clear immigration and customs just outside of town. We were still more than 250 miles from the Algeria–Niger border, but in the middle of the desert there was no official border procedure. It was done in the oasis town. Mid-morning we drove through this checkpoint. During the two-hour procedure, the temperature rose to the high 90s.

When we were finally ready to depart, two of our vehicles wouldn't start. Gérard, our mechanic, found their carburetors plugged. He checked the auxiliary oil-bath air filters. They were about one quart low, causing the plugged carburetors. Just beyond the customs barrier, at 12:30 PM, we lined up all the vehicles and checked them. Five needed their carburetor cleaned and oil added to their auxiliary air filter. Fortunately we were only one mile outside of Tamanrasset. If these vehicle breakdowns had happened after we were deep in the desert, we would not have had enough oil with us to fill the air filters as well as our engines.

After getting permission from the customs police, we returned to town and bought additional oil. Because it was 6:30 PM by the time all the vehicles were repaired, we traveled only twenty miles before setting up camp that night. As I drifted off to sleep, I thanked the Lord for watching over us. He was truly keeping His promise to "make a way for us in the desert." But even so, our desert crossing was far from over.

ELEVEN

Crossing the Desert

IT WAS on our fifth day of travel out of Tamanrasset that we got lost, a day after we crossed into Niger. We dead-ended in a field of huge sand dunes. Since leaving Tamanrasset, there had been no clearly defined track through the sea of sand. Now, having lost our way, I consulted with Keith, who had been leading our convoy. If we didn't correct our course quickly, our vehicles could get stuck in the middle of the desert with no fuel, miles away from an oasis town and a water source. Just when Keith and I agreed that we should head west, to our surprise two Tuareg boys came out from among the sand dunes, waving to us. They didn't speak English or French, but through gestures we were able to ask which way the road was. The older boy pointed east, the opposite direction to what Keith and I had chosen.

I gestured an invitation for the boys to come direct us in our vehicle. The smaller boy refused, but the older one agreed. I drove as he pointed, and the other vehicles followed. He gave precise directions, indicating which way around each sand dune. He knew the desert like his backyard. *The younger boy must be rejoining his family by foot*, I thought. *He must also know the desert well.*

Our guide looked about twelve years old. I could see white patches of lice in his bushy, jet-black hair. *He must not be an angel. God wouldn't allow lice in heaven*, I thought. His worn, turquoise-blue robe hung over a tattered pair of gray pants that sagged over his homemade tire-tread sandals. His gentle smile was contagious. Knowing I couldn't understand his words, he communicated by pointing with his hands. After driving a couple of miles, we spotted a marker post. Passing a second one, we saw a woman with two small children up ahead on foot. The boy pointed and smiled. That was his family. His mother wore a dark robe that reached to her feet. A black headscarf shaded her from the intense sun.

She smiled pleasantly, and greeted us in an African language none of us understood. We expressed our thanks to her and her son with some canned goods, water, and inadequate hand gestures. As we drove away waving good-bye, one of my French-speaking students, remembering *The Little Prince* by Antoine de Saint Exupéry, nicknamed this boy our "Little Prince."

I relaxed and thanked God as we again passed marker posts. I marveled at how He had rescued us from near disaster. But I didn't dwell on this too long—I still had to concentrate on driving. We needed to get to our next destination alive.

Around noon we spotted a tall thorn bush surrounded by a man in a white robe and turban, with his wives and children, sitting in the shade on blue and brown blankets. A camel and a couple of beige canvas tents propped up by an assortment of wooden poles punctuated the area behind them. The man invited us to drink the traditional three cups of mint tea. Sitting on one of the blankets under the thorn bush, I immediately discovered and removed a twig sprouting sharp, two-inch thorns.

While the tea was being prepared, one of the mothers asked if we had medication for her children's infections. The three nurses in our group began to treat the children's runny, diseased, fly-bitten eyes. I helped Christa, one of our nurses, with an eight-year-old boy. His right eye was already blind and the lid was swollen over it. His left eye was intact but diseased. We treated him as best we could, but the experience troubled me deeply. I reflected on how we were so blessed with medical care in the West, so far removed from these precious people. What would I do, I wondered, if my daughter were in this same situation? What must this mother and father have felt as they saw their son slowly going blind?

As I sat thinking, the mint tea was finally ready, and we shared our noon meal with them. The man also gave us some warm camel's milk. Most of us winced at the taste of the strong, pungent flavor. As we ate, two other men arrived on camelback. We gave a Gospel of John in Arabic to our new friend. Immediately sitting down, he began reading it out loud, chanting as he read. The two newly arrived men sat and listened intently. All were very warm and kind. The Lord had opened this door to minister to people in the middle of the Sahara.

Early evening the following day we reached Agadez. All of our gasoline cans were empty, and our gas tanks were nearly dry. After digging vehicles out of the sand a total of seventy-seven times in those six days, we were so grateful to finally see this little oasis town of eight thousand inhabitants.

"Look," shouted Lidia as we arrived at the outskirts of Agadez. We all burst out laughing as we encountered our first stop sign in several weeks of driving—hand painted and fastened to a stick. To one side was a rider on horseback waiting to cross, so I dutifully stopped my vehicle, waiting my turn at this intersection of two desert tracks.

We checked into the campground and found the house of a missionary couple to whom the Lausanne center had forwarded our mail. From 10:00 PM till 1:00 AM we read our first mail in over five weeks. Judi wrote that she enjoyed working with the student prayer groups and arranging the morning coffee breaks for the staff. Doing hospitality brought her pleasure. Encouragement from home breathed new hope into us all.

"I think we must be through the worst of it," I heard Keith say the following morning, a day of rest for us. I certainly hoped so. It did seem that our prayers were now shifting—from asking God for protection to asking him to direct our ministry in West Africa.

The next day we prepared for our final 374-mile, three-day desert crossing to Tahoua. This would bring us into the savannah near the borders of Niger, Burkina Faso, and Nigeria. Several of our team filtered water into our water containers, others filled our five-gallon metal gasoline cans at a service station, and others purchased food. That evening the food crew bought everyone shish kabobs prepared at the local market over an open fire. One of our team thought something tasted wrong with her shish kabob, so I ate hers as well as mine.

The next morning we registered our itinerary at the local police station and departed. About mid-morning my stomach began gurgling, followed by the runs. By early afternoon I was vomiting every ten to fifteen minutes. The driver would stop the van as I dropped out onto the sand on all fours, retching. After an hour of dry heaves and diarrhea in the 104-degree heat, I was so dehydrated I couldn't walk, and I almost lost consciousness. Someone had to drag me behind a bush and then come and get me when I called. I was desperately thirsty but couldn't hold down any liquid.

"You probably got food poisoning from those shish kabobs," said one of the nurses. "I don't think it's wise to go on any longer."

Keith and Don decided to stop and set up camp. Others were also sick.

The tent I lay in under the midday sun felt like the inside of an oven. Sometimes I heard voices around me, and at other times I wasn't sure where I was or what was happening. I came to full awareness occasionally and felt moist towels on my forehead. I tried to drink a little, but nothing stayed down. At half past midnight, for the first time, I was able to hold down a few swallows of tea. Like a dream come true, it began to ease my aching pain and unquenchable thirst. The next morning, though I felt very weak, I was doing better, as were the others who had been sick. We broke camp and departed.

During this segment we encountered dried-up bushes sprouting sharp, two-inch thorns. Avoiding them for the sake of our tires meant going through some very deep ruts. The landscape changed farther south, when we entered the savannah, with tall dry grass and brush. On the third day we began to encounter people, at first desert nomads, and then we began seeing the smiling faces of West Africans. Little children came running out of their mud-brick dwellings, chasing after us, waving and laughing. We created quite an event when we slowed and drove through the middle of each encampment of five or six huts.

Around 2:30 in the afternoon we arrived at our intended destination, Tahoua, only to discover that the village had been out of gasoline for over two weeks. Thankfully, we had filled our jerry cans sufficiently at Agadez, so we decided to press on the additional one hundred miles to the next village. Late that evening we arrived, refilled our gasoline, and spent the night.

The next day as we approached Niamey, the capital of Niger, we encountered something that nearly brought tears to my eyes—a short stretch of paved road leading into the city. A tangible sign that we had achieved our first goal. We had crossed the Sahara.

After two and a half days in Niamey, our three schools prepared to depart in different directions. We said good-bye to Keith and Marian Warrington, who with the German school would cross into Nigeria, and to Don and Evey Heckman, who with the British school would drive down to Ghana. Having been through so much together, we found it hard to separate. God had helped us overcome daunting challenges, and in doing so He formed a bond in our hearts.

We would not see them again on this trip; all three schools would return to Europe separately. I thought about our Swiss school, which had fought so many battles already. I wondered how things would be different being on our own and what new challenges could be waiting for us in French West Africa.

TWELVE

Attack under the Baobab Trees

FROM Niamey, once again leaving the paved road behind us, we pressed on to Ouagadougou, the capital of Burkina Faso, where we stopped for vehicle repairs. With our various delays, we were already over a week behind the schedule we had telegrammed to the missionaries we planned to work with. I hoped this wouldn't create problems for us along the way, but unfortunately it did. In Ouagadougou we learned that a missionary was expecting us to hold a Sunday service the next day in Bobo-Dioulasso, 220 miles away. Another friend at the American Evangelical Mission invited us to hold a service for him that evening in Ouagadougou.

Travel in Burkina Faso was painfully slow because of difficult road conditions and a border war with Mali that imposed continual police controls and a nightly military curfew. Calling the missionary in Bobo-Dioulasso, I explained that if we left at 4:00 AM the next morning, we could make it to Bobo-Dioulasso before 10:00 AM. We went to the military post, getting permission to leave before the nightly curfew was lifted.

Sunday morning at 4:10 AM we drove out of town and through the military police barrier. As we bounced over the rugged, potholed dirt road, one of our vehicles broke down. We sent two vehicles ahead to Bobo-Dioulasso and worked to tow the other one. Unfortunately, none of our vehicles arrived in time for the service, much to the chagrin of the missionary. Not only had we missed that service, but I found out we had missed twelve hundred youth at a rally he had organized the week before. We had been unaware of this event, which was organized when we were in the desert without any means of communication. It hurt to miss such a good opportunity to minister to African young people. I could sense the disappointment of others created by our delayed arrival. But in spite of perpetual wind-blown dust, we were very grateful for actual beds in guest rooms and cold showers instead of tents and a bowl of water to wash with.

We waited another week in Bobo-Dioulasso while Gérard, our mechanic, with the help of Hubert and Michel, two of our drivers, rebuilt the engine that had died on the road. Tension rose within the team again, being stuck where we had missed several ministry opportunities. Occasional biting remarks or sour looks cut me to the heart. Each day I committed the team to the Lord and tried to make the most of our "lost time." The team had opportunity to minister to a church choir, a women's group, a youth center, and various classes in a primary school.

On Wednesday morning we met in small groups, in which God highlighted the need for team unity. That afternoon I shared my excitement with the team about our upcoming ministry in Ivory Coast. "I know you are as frustrated as I am by the struggles and challenges we've faced along the way, but now the best part of our outreach is about to begin." A few negative murmurs came in response, but mostly expressions of hope. Gérard said he thought the engine would be finished and reinstalled in our van by noon the next day, so we told the team to pack and prepare for departure the following day.

On Thursday the engine was still not running, and we delayed our departure another day. I shared in a team meeting about the state of negativity we seemed to be in and the importance of working on unity. That evening, when we met again, several of the team lashed out vehemently over all the delays and problems. I felt like I had been punched in the stomach. I knew these were reactions to real frustrations; we really had had difficulties along the way. But the criticism still hurt. I didn't want to strike back in anger or self-defense, so I just ended the meeting and slipped away to pray.

Around 11:30 PM news came to me that our motor was repaired and installed. Meeting with André and Marie Christine, my two staff members, I asked the Lord whether we should delay our departure to deal with the explosion in the team or depart the next day. Going back to my daily Bible reading, I reread Proverbs 20. Verse 22 stood out. "Do not say, 'I'll pay you back for this wrong!' Wait for the LORD, and he will deliver you." I sensed the Lord was saying to me, "Depart. Leave this situation to Me. I will deliver you." So I prayed, "Lord, I place the team in Your hands." Then we got word out to the team that the motor was repaired and we would leave the next morning.

At 8:30 Friday morning, February 21, we departed for the little bush village of Bouroum-Bouroum, still in Burkina Faso but six or seven hours away. Our plan was to visit a Swiss missionary who worked there. We had been told the dirt road passing by that village had less pronounced washboard undulations in it than the main road to Ivory Coast. I squinted through my dust-streaked windshield as I drove along the dirt track crossing the drought-stricken savannah. Occasionally I saw a lone baobab tree sticking above the dried brush. These trees were tall and grotesquely thick and were called "the tree that grows upside down." Their tops looked more like thick, stunted root systems than branches.

Hoping for some shade from the 104-degree heat, I stopped our caravan for lunch by a clump of gnarled baobab trees. Clouds of reddish dust engulfed my van as our caravan pulled in behind me. The team emerged, weary from four hours of pounding on the pitted dirt road. The air was still and hot, only disturbed by the song of cicadas and the cooing of doves. Flies buzzed, gnats hovered, and an occasional grasshopper jumped across this parched area of shade. The team slowly moved into action. Lidia, our Sicilian team member, spread old army blankets and tablecloths on the ground and gathered a few wilted flowers for our "table." Evelyne prepared our lunch of bread, canned sardines, and liver paste. (Lack of refrigeration didn't leave us many options for food.) Individual conversations and excited chatter echoed everywhere.

While we finished eating, the girls filed behind a large baobab tree across the track for a "restroom" stop. Suddenly screams shattered the stillness, shrieks of utter terror and panic. The hair on the back of my neck bristled, and cold chills ran up and down my spine. My heart pounded against my rib cage and throbbed in my ears. My mind raced. *Cobras? Vipers? Wild Animals?*

In near unison those of us sitting on the blankets stood and sprinted toward the cries. Instantly I was enveloped by a thick, angry cloud of loudly buzzing, dive-bombing insects slamming into my face and arms. Instinctively I closed my eyes and madly brushed the insects away. A hot, fiery stinger pierced my cheek. My arms flailed frantically, trying to keep other insects from stinging me, but more stings followed as the insects all declared war on us. They were frenzied, attacking bees—dreaded African killer bees—in a swarm the size of a house.

I ran blindly, anywhere away from the high-pitched roar of thousands of angry, darting bees. I beat the air. I had to keep those creatures away from my face and neck. At the outer limits of my senses, through the overpowering din, I became aware of other screams and people running.

Among the voices I heard Christa crying out, "I'm allergic to bees! I'm allergic to bees!" Her desperation stopped me. Rebuking my panic, I ran toward her, grabbed her arm, and pulled her away from the infested tree. We were just emerging from the thickest part of the cloud of attacking bees when I heard another hysterical voice. "My father died this way. My father died this way," Daisy, one of our Swiss students, was repeating. I pointed Christa down the road to a small group of people gathering about two hundred yards away, and ran back toward Daisy. She continued to babble about her father dying from a bee sting. The bees around her attacked me, too, and chased us as we ran down the road. It felt like several hot needles piercing my face and neck. We ran and ran until, finally, no more bees bombarded us.

Rushing to our team, I saw Lidia stretched out on the ground. She was covered with bee stingers still wriggling and pumping venom—on her eyelids and ears, all over her face and neck, and all over her arms and hands. Bees buzzed, caught in her long black hair. Several people quickly but carefully removed more than eighty stingers from her and cautiously pulled the bees from her hair.

She gasped in a strained, halting whisper, "I . . . can't . . . breathe." Then her eyes rolled back and her head fell into the reddish dust of the roadway. My heart pounded against my heaving rib cage. I knelt in the dirt track wanting desperately to pray, but I couldn't calm my thoughts. A sense of fear and inadequacy swept over me. There was no one nearby I could turn to for help. I felt totally alone. If God didn't come through, Lidia, and possibly several other team members, could die.

I caught my breath and forced myself to pray. What came out of my mouth was the last thing I expected to hear. I heard myself praying, "God, this crisis isn't Your fault. I'm not mad at You. What You have made is good and beautiful: the snow-capped mountains, the forests, the desert we crossed, the savannah, the baobab trees, and even the bees. Thank You for the beauty of all of Your creation." I couldn't believe my ears. I was thanking God for the whole creation, even the bees! But the more I thanked Him, the calmer I felt. Slowly my panic lifted.

Then, deep down in my spirit, a righteous anger arose in my heart, indignation at the devil and at death. He was *not* going to win this one. Words began to come from deep within, carrying a forceful authority. They were not being formed in my mind. Instead of talking to God now, I heard myself taking authority over the devil and commanding his power and attack to be broken. Then I called on God to heal Lidia.

While I knelt there praying, a large, gray transport truck pulled up and stopped in a cloud of dust, the first vehicle I had seen in several hours. A hitchhiker jumped out and walked over to us. He introduced himself as a worker with the public health department. As he surveyed our situation, he offered the unbelievable. "I have an injection of something that might help." Seeing Lidia unconscious, he said, "It's too late for her." I was stunned. Without helping her, he walked over to two other girls who were lying on their sides vomiting. One had been stung over forty times, the other over twenty-five times. He gave them both a shot. When the truck driver honked the horn, the health care worker scurried back, and the truck drove away.

I turned back to Lidia's unconscious form. She urgently needed help. One of our nurses fought her way to a van through the swarm still hovering over our picnic site. Grabbing the medical kit, she rushed back to Lidia and gave her a shot of antihistamine. One of the guys covered himself with a blanket and also reached a van, driving it back to us. It bounced from one side of the road to the other as he jerked the steering wheel, ducking angry bees. Two other drivers covered themselves with gloves and djellabas found in the baggage of the first van to get the other vehicles. As they put on these coverings, I recalled having thought that these purchases in Morocco would become useless excess material to carry on the trip. *Lord, I apologize for my rash judgment. Thank You for your faithfulness in even the tiniest details.*

By the time we situated Lidia on the back seat of the first van, the other vans had arrived, and people loaded into them. One of the nurses and I sat in front of Lidia to keep an eye on her. Now 4:30 PM, we hurried off toward the missionary infirmary in Bouroum-Bouroum, still a couple of hours away. As I silently prayed, our nurse bathed Lidia's forehead with a cool, damp cloth.

An hour later Lidia stirred. Jerking her arm, she slowly mumbled, "Cut...off...my...hair." My heart jumped. A sense of relief, rejoicing, and fatigue swept over me. She mumbled again, "Cut off my hair."

"It's okay, Lidia," I assured her. "We already pulled the bees out of your hair."

Her eyes opened, and she leaned up on her elbow. I asked her what she remembered of the last few hours. "I remember not being able to breathe. I felt my life leaving me. As soon as you began to pray, it was as if a cool breeze swept over me and I was able to breathe. But, Joe, I couldn't thank God for all His creation. Some of His creation almost killed me! Then I remember hearing a voice say, 'It's too late for her.' In my heart I cried out to God, 'No, Lord, that's not fair to my mother.' My father didn't want me to come on this trip and said he would hold my mother responsible for my life. It seems unbelievable, but I heard Him answer me, 'I am the God of the living, not the dead.' I clung to that word. I knew I would make it."

An hour later we arrived at a tiny mud-hut village rejoicing. We blurted out our story to the missionaries, one of whom had invited us to come when she passed through Bobo-Dioulasso the week before. Christa had been stung twelve times but had no allergic reaction. Lidia showed no signs of swelling, but the rest of us were quite a sight with our swollen and painful bumps. Our Swiss missionary friend, amazed that Lidia had lived through this, told us of another foreigner who had disturbed a hive of bees. He died after being stung over forty times.

I fell into my sleeping bag that night more exhausted than I had felt in ages. Relief washed over me. The Christian life is not deliverance from trouble but deliverance in trouble. "Thank You, Lord, for calming my fears and sparing Lidia's life. In spite of that bee attack, You are good," I prayed.

I realized the battles we faced would not be easy if we expected to break through to the spiritual needs of French West Africa. The enemy didn't want us to open a doorway of ministry for YWAM there, our first spiritual beachhead or foothold. But God was there to help us. As Psalm 37:20 told me, "The LORD's enemies will . . . vanish like smoke." The "brick wall" of killer bees was only a smoke screen. When we resisted the enemy, he left.

I also realized the devil's attacks came when we were most vulnerable. Disunity in our group left a wide open door for the enemy. I felt so lonely and so far away from my friends in Switzerland. But God was always with us, and he was greater than any attack the enemy could send. Those attacks dissipated quickly with God's help. This was still God's outreach. He was still making a way in this (spiritual) desert.

I would soon see that this harrowing day was the beginning of a positive turning point for some of the discontented students.

THIRTEEN

French West Africa

"DON'T go near that big tree. Blood sacrifices are made there," warned our Swiss missionary friend.

"What kind of blood sacrifices?" someone gasped.

"Chicken blood, not human blood," the missionary responded. "But still, stay away."

This warning served as a grim reminder of the spiritual needs of the animistic tribes of sub-Saharan Africa. Our host showed us around the Lobi village of Bouroum-Bouroum, a collection of huts made of irregularly formed, handmade mud bricks. On each of the flat-roofed huts, millet was laid out to dry. After visiting the village clinic, we departed about noon to continue our journey to Ivory Coast.

Soon my stomach growled; it was lunchtime. Up ahead I saw several baobab trees clumped around the dirt track. It looked like a good spot to stop, but the bee attack the day before was still vivid in all of our minds. As we pulled up to the trees, I felt a knot in my stomach that had nothing to do with my hunger. I saw apprehension on the faces of the others as I stepped out of our van and walked into the shade, listening carefully for buzzing sounds. When I didn't hear any, I motioned for the others to come. Some of our team wouldn't budge until we prayed. So I raised my voice, "Lord, please protect us as we sit under these trees. Place Your angels around us. Hold us carefully in Your hands. And thank You for the food You provided. Bless it to bring strength and nourishment to us. Thank You for Your gracious provision." When lunch was ready, we ate quickly, still not wanting to remain too long under those baobab trees.

The next day we stopped for lunch in another grove of trees. It appeared safe enough, but soon after we stepped out to stretch our legs, we were swarmed by hundreds of tiny gnats. Trying to swat them away, I breathed in a couple that caught in the back of my throat. Another flew up my nose. Running back to our vans, we ate lunch with the windows rolled up in spite of the heat.

A couple of hours later we completed border-crossing formalities into Ivory Coast. After a journey of over 5,500 miles through seven countries we had reached our initial goal. I hoped that now the struggles of this long trek were at an end. That afternoon the steering tie bar on my van broke. It was impossible to drive, so we stopped at a nearby town. We were directed to the vice governor of the region, who arranged housing for us while the van was being repaired.

As I lay in bed that night, I tried out French words to describe the events of the last few days, like a teenager trying on clothes at a mall. After two months with this French-speaking team, my mind had settled into the French language. My quiet musings were in French, as was my Bible meditation. Even my dreams were in French. I thanked the Lord for helping me connect with the team, not just in heart, but also in language.

Early the next morning two guys, Alan and Gérard, went into town to purchase a new tie bar. They returned very excited, carrying a used tie bar.

"You should have seen it, Joe!" Alan exclaimed.

"Seen what?"

"We went into town and couldn't find a tie bar anywhere."

"What's so exciting about that?" I asked. "Where did you get that one?"

"Someone told us about an old abandoned VW van just outside of town," Alan continued. "It was totally burned out and turned on its side. But examining it more closely, we found the only part not burned was the tie bar. It's a miracle! I love seeing God take care of us."

While they installed the tie bar, the rest of the team met in small groups and talked about what God was doing among us. In the women's group Lidia shared, "I felt a growing tension in our team. I told the Lord, 'We'll never have team unity.' Then the killer bees attacked. The Lord healed me of the bee stings, but much more than that, He showed me how important it was for me to be committed to Him and to our team. I needed the guys who risked their lives to rescue me. I realized that I'm accountable for my behavior and actions. As we work out our own spiritual problems, I believe God will start bringing unity to us." The students prayed for each other, and God began the healing process for several that day.

The African young people from the local high school asked to spend time with us. Getting out the map of West Africa, we told them about our trip and what God had been doing on our journey.

"Why did you make such a long journey to come to West Africa?" one young man asked.

"Because God loves Africa and called us to bring His good news to people here," I replied.

As we spoke about God's concern for Africa, we could see hunger in their eyes and hear it in their questions. We told them God wanted to lead them into adventures with Him. They asked about Christian beliefs and how they could personally experience God. We broke into smaller groups so that more of them could ask questions. One of our team told me later, "We were assailed with questions, but we had answers to give. We saw God do great things in several of their lives as they opened their hearts to him. Hallelujah!" It felt wonderful to finally begin fulfilling the ministry for which we came to West Africa.

The next day our vans entered the West African rainforest. For the first time in weeks we felt humidity. Stopping under a canopy of huge trees, we listened to bird and animal calls that sounded like the sound-track of an old *Tarzan* movie. A cheer went up from those in my van when we drove onto asphalt again. "Wow, I'd forgotten how smooth paved road feels," someone said.

That evening we arrived in Abidjan, then the capital of Ivory Coast. This huge metropolitan area, the first we had seen in nearly two months, resembled a modern European city. We searched for a public telephone to call the missionaries but could not find one that worked. We drove around for some time, hoping to find the Evangelical Mission station on our own. Suddenly a vehicle pulled up alongside our four extremely dusty vans, and a woman stuck her head out the window. "Are you the group from Switzerland that is coming to the Evangelical Mission?"

I slowed and shouted back, "Yes, we are. Do you know where it is? We're a little lost."

She smiled, "Yes, I'm one of the missionaries who has been waiting for you. Follow me."

When we got to the station, we were told quite a bit of our mail had arrived. But the pastor in whose office it was stored was not there. So after weeks without mail, we had to wait till the next morning. One of our guys said, "Is there any way we can spring the lock to the office?"

"Whoa," I said. "We've waited this long. A little longer won't kill us." But I knew exactly how he felt. I wanted so badly to read my mail from Judi and Lisa.

The following morning the pastor came, unlocked his office, and gave us our mail. Proverbs 25:25 says, "Like cold water to a weary soul is good news from a distant land." That's how it was for us. Our morning was instantly refreshed with news from home. I so enjoyed hearing from Judi. Tears of joy ran down more than one face as people read in silence.

That afternoon our team sang Scripture choruses for the dedication of a new mission radio studio built to serve French West Africa. Pastors and church members came from all over West Africa to be present. This made my task of rearranging our ministry schedule much easier.

Exhausted from two months of travel, we took a day off at the beach. We chose to go to a place where we could picnic, though we heard the ocean was unsafe for swimming. Waves hit partway up the steep slope of the shoreline and quickly receded back into the murky depths. Peering into the ocean, I could not see the bottom; the water was immediately deep. I felt uneasy. Then one of our students, strolling along the shore, was caught by a wave and swept out to sea. I began despairing that we would never reach her, when all of a sudden God sent a wave that threw her back into our reach, and we pulled her out of the water. She collapsed on the sand, shivering with fear. It took me a moment to break her vice-like grip on my hand. We were quite shaken as we spread our picnic lunch on the beach at least a hundred feet from the water. Though we had heard that Africa's shoreline could be treacherous, we now knew why. Conversation over lunch was subdued.

Later I reflected over what had transpired. One of our team who had seemed withdrawn from us, almost lost in the waves, now reconnected with us emotionally after her rescue.

After the physical and emotional drain of traveling and the incident at the beach, our team finally was able to settle into the new surroundings and regain focus. I transitioned leadership to André, who would be in charge of the ministry time in Ivory Coast. They would be reaching out to churches, youth groups, and schools in several districts of Abidjan. They would also invite people to meetings where they would sing and testify before showing an evangelistic movie.

I had arranged to return to Switzerland for a week to be with Judi and Lisa. I went to the airport, wait-listed only, and God opened a place on a fully booked flight. That night, in just a few short hours, the plane flew over the same route that had taken us two months to drive. I slept the whole way over the desert this time and awakened just as we prepared to land in Geneva. My heart quickened as I realized my pregnant wife was now just minutes away. I wondered how Judi would react to the stories of the challenges we had faced. Would she worry about me returning to Africa?

I hurried down the plane's stairs hardly fazed by the flying snowflakes and the cold wind that penetrated my thin, blue windbreaker and baggy, black polyester pants that I had washed one too many times in African streams. Going from a fast walk to a slow run, I hurried through immigration and, without stopping at baggage claim and customs, ran straight into Judi's arms.

"I missed you so much," I said, drawing her close. "You really look pretty in that green maternity dress!" She flashed a glowing smile.

Lisa was at home sleeping, so Judi and I talked nonstop on the forty-five-minute drive home. Across the lake, the French Alps stood like white citadels. What a change from the tropical rainforest I had left the day before and the scorched desert I had recently crossed.

The next evening I reported on our Africa trip to new students. Among other stories, I told about getting lost in the Sahara and how a young boy, coming from behind a sand dune, had shown us the way back to the marked trail.

After the meeting I met a South African student named Elgonda Brunkhorst. "I was very interested in your story about being lost in the Sahara," she said. "But weren't there two children?"

How does she know that? I only spoke about the one boy, I thought. "Yes, there were two children, but only one got in and showed us the way. How did you know there were two?"

She smiled. "A few weeks ago I participated in a student intercession group. We asked God to show us what He wanted us to pray for. We waited, listening. A long silence followed. Someone sensed the word *Africa*. Then I saw a picture in my mind of sand that seemed to stretch on forever. Dust billowed behind a Volkswagen van not following any road. The prayer leader felt this applied to your outreach team."

"Yes," I said. "Out in the Sahara, the sand stretches as far as the eye can see."

"The group started praying," Elgonda continued. "We felt you were lost, because the van was not following any road. A second picture came to my mind. In it, two children played among the rocks. We asked the Lord to send an angel to lead you back to the road. God's presence gave us details of what to pray. That's why I got so excited hearing you share about a child helping you find your way. We prayed the morning of February 3. What date were you lost?"

I looked in my journal, which I had brought with me, and was stunned by what I saw. "February 3!" I replied excitedly. "God led you to pray for us during the very time we were lost!"

Later I thought more about that prayer meeting and about getting lost in the desert. Our team really had been in danger. God had led that group to pray for us and had protected us from disaster. I recalled Isaiah 43:19, the scripture God had used five months earlier to reassure me that this was His trip and that He would be with us. "I am making a way in the desert." I knew God was watching and would continue to watch over us. I relaxed as I thought about rejoining my team in West Africa in a few days.

The week in Switzerland ended all too quickly. Sooner than I wanted to, I said good-bye to Judi and Lisa and found myself sitting on an airplane flying back to West Africa. As I flew over the Sahara at thirty-five thousand feet, I thought, *It looks so easy from up here to travel over those thread-like trails down on the dull beige desert floor below.* Getting off the plane in Abidjan, Ivory Coast, I felt like I was pushing through a wall of humidity.

On my first Sunday back I preached at an evangelical church in Abidjan. Jean Glao, the African pastor, had experienced a personal revival in his heart and was passionate in transmitting it to his people. The congregation responded with much enthusiasm to worship and the truths of God's Word. The Lord led us to encourage Jean as he faced outside opposition to the move of God in his church. Having overcome so many trials ourselves, I could see that the Lord was now using us to encourage others in their times of testing.

The following day most of the team departed for the interior with André, while I remained in Abidjan with one of our broken-down vans and four of our team. Two worked on rebuilding the engine, two worked on travel arrangements to Mali and Senegal, and one began writing to our friends about our changed schedule. It was too late in the season to try to drive back through the Sahara. Temperatures were already rising dangerously high. Each time I called our contacts in Mali, I spent an hour at the downtown post office waiting to get an available phone line. Working on our return arrangements to Switzerland by plane from Dakar, Senegal, I could make reservations but not buy tickets. We needed to sell three vans to pay for our plane tickets.

One very humid night I lay all sticky on top of my sleeping bag, under my mosquito net, wishing for a slight breeze to pass under my tin-roofed, one-room dwelling. The humidity was stifling. I watched several eight-inch lizards cling to the walls. They ate big flying cockroaches, but they did nothing to eliminate the myriad of malaria mosquitoes humming in the air. These annoyances were new to us from Europe but were part of the daily fabric of life for West Africans. Looking at our struggles in that context gave me new compassion for the people here. I hoped that others on our team would also see things in that light.

Relational tensions in our group had arisen again. One of our students, whom I had kept with me in Abidjan, was continually venomous in her murmurings and verbal attacks about the difficulties of this trip. I had a frank discussion with her of how her attitude affected others, and she opened her heart to the Lord. She asked for His help regarding some problems she had had with people in her teens, which she felt were the roots of her current struggles with God and others.

I called André and the team up-country in the city of Yamoussoukro. They had been ministering through singing, testimonies, and "round table" discussions with young people in high schools run by various missions. The team also encouraged churches and youth groups and challenged a group of Bible school students with the need for African missionaries in Europe and other parts of the world. Personal contact with African young people was very encouraging. Many were touched by the fact that our team members each had a profession (nurses, teachers, mechanics, etc.) and could have done something else besides mission work in Africa. André's report encouraged me.

The five of us rejoined the rest of the team in northern Ivory Coast. I was able to sell one of the vans, so nineteen of us, along with our luggage and camping equipment, squeezed into our three remaining vans. Traveling to Mali, we had opportunities to minister to youth in Sikasso and Bamako. We discovered there was no longer a road between Bamako, Mali's capital city, and Senegal; the bridges had washed away, and we didn't have four-wheel-drive vehicles to ford the rivers. The only possibility was to load the three vans and ourselves onto a train that went weekly from Bamako to Dakar. We were told it could take two or three weeks to get space on the train, but God worked a miracle, and within five days we loaded our three vans onto a flatcar for the journey.

We traveled third class on the eighteen-and-a-half-hour trip to Tamacounda, the first train station in eastern Senegal. We stood without seats for the first eight hours. The aisles were piled high with bundles, goats, and chickens. I found a little spot to sit on the steps that descended out the open door. While I sat there watching the landscape fly by, one of the African mothers took her toddler to the bottom step to relieve himself. Some of the spray hit my feet. Finally, enough people descended that we could sit in actual seats. At each train stop vendors flocked along the track, reaching into the train windows with food items and water. As a precaution, we told the team not to touch any of it. We filtered and carried our own water. Though ours was tepid and the vendors' was fresh and cool, there were too many risks in drinking it. We arrived at 2:00 AM the next morning and found several rooms in a simple hotel that looked like a boarding house from an old black-and-white Western movie.

From Tamacounda we went to minister with a missionary couple we knew in a tiny village called Kédougou, a seven-hour drive south through the bush. We arrived during the period of initiation rights for boys, and the spiritual climate was tense. One day a witch doctor attacked me as I walked along a path in the village. Wearing an ugly black mask and a grotesque mass of tree bark and fibers, he looked like a huge hedgehog. I could only tell he was human by the sound of his voice as he shouted something in a language I couldn't understand. Thankfully, when he grabbed me, I was engulfed by the mass of bark and was too close for him to get a good swing at me. The local missionary yelled something and pulled us apart.

That night, several team members woke up in a cold sweat from demonic nightmares. Praying together, we resisted and bound the enemy's attacks in the name of Jesus, quoting James 4:7: "Submit yourselves, then, to God. Resist the devil, and he will flee from you," and Colossians 2:15: "And having disarmed the powers and authorities, he [Jesus] made a public spectacle of them, triumphing over them by the cross." Then, in the name of Jesus we declared His victory over these attacks. After that night, with God's help we were able to share our faith and minister positively in the village.

Throughout our time in West Africa, we had many opportunities to speak at church services and youth meetings in Ivory Coast, Mali, and now in Senegal. The thing we enjoyed most was talking individually with African young people; they were so full of questions and wanted hope for their future. I could see the Lord using them to touch their world for God. My vision of going to French West Africa was being fulfilled, and foundations were being laid to do more mission work in the future.

We had reservations for one van, packed with camping gear, to depart by ship on April 12 and the team to fly back to Europe on April 13. We needed to sell the other two vans to pay for our plane tickets. But as we made arrangements to leave, one thought nagged my mind: had our team worked through its internal tensions? I didn't want the team returning to Europe in disunity.

FOURTEEN

The Battle for Unity

WE HAD now been on the road more than fourteen weeks, having traveled over eight thousand miles, and every day our thoughts were turning toward our return to Europe. On April 7 an advance team traveled to Dakar to repair and put two of our vans up for sale and complete arrangements to put our third one on a ship to France. The rest of the team and I stayed for a few more days to minister in Kédougou before departing. We arrived in Dakar just two days before the cargo ship, M/V *Massalia*, departed with our van stuffed with all our camping equipment. We were unable to sell the other two vans in time for our April 13 reservations on a charter flight to Switzerland, so we rescheduled for April 17. With all this uncertainty and change, I sensed tension in the team again.

We tried to redeem the time, taking opportunities to minister in churches and youth groups during that week. Meanwhile, our mechanic, Gérard, with the help of Hubert and Michel, began extensive work on our two Volkswagen buses. We had learned that vehicles needing a lot of repairs typically sold for 100 to 200 USD while those in good shape could fetch 1500 to 2000 USD. We rebuilt the engine in the blue van, repaired the body, and repainted it, and then began working on the white one, rebuilding the engine and doing body work. People regularly came by to look at our vehicles, but no one offered to buy them. When we failed to sell our vans by April 17, we again had to cancel our flight reservations. Once more discouragement set in. To avoid raising hopes and dashing them again, we did not reschedule flight reservations, deciding to wait until we actually sold the vans.

I called together my two staff, André and Marie Christine, for prayer. We asked the Lord for understanding about why we were having so much trouble selling our vehicles. While we waited in prayer, Marie Christine spoke up. "I saw a picture in my mind of a ship at the port in Dakar. As I looked more closely, I could see that most of our team had boarded it, but a few were still on the dock. Then it raised its gangway and set sail with some of our people still on the dock."

"Could this be a picture of the spiritual condition of our team?" I asked. "We know that not all have fully entered into what God wants for their lives." As this understanding settled in my heart, I blurted out, "We can't leave anyone behind spiritually! Lord, please stop the ship. Stop it until all of our people are able to board."

"I see that picture again," Marie Christine said. "The ship has stopped and the gangway has come back down on the dock again." Then the picture ended. At that time we didn't fully understand the implication of our decision to ask God to "stop the ship," but we would discover it soon enough.

As work continued on the vans, I prayed for and spoke with those who still needed a spiritual breakthrough. Days passed, and I saw no change in their hearts. I pleaded with God for answers, as more potential buyers came and went and the team became more demoralized.

Then one of our team members, Marc, became ill and had to be taken to the hospital, where he was diagnosed with hepatitis. This is an easily transmitted disease, especially through contaminated water, and I was alarmed about the threat to our team. Since we were still filtering all of our drinking water, I wondered how he could have been infected. In talking with him I discovered that he had purchased some of the cool, nonfiltered water from one of the vendors along the train route we had traversed weeks before. From his hospital bed he said to me, "This is a hard way to learn to listen to what I've been told."

Two Africans came to look at our vans. Things looked positive, but they also backed out.

When I met for prayer that night with André and Marie Christine, the weight of all we faced finally came out. "I miss Judi and Lisa so much I feel the pain physically. I want so desperately to get back to them." I began to sob uncontrollably. My two friends prayed for me and my family. When I could pray, I cried out, "Father, please release Your love across the miles to my family, including our unborn child. You know how much I want to be with them." In that moment I sensed God's grace again to keep on fighting.

At the end of the week we drove our two renovated vans to the beach. When we were leaving at the end of the day, the white one would not start. We towed it to a garage and found that the rebuilt crankcase sold to us by a parts dealer was defective. Oil could not get to the engine parts, and our newly rebuilt engine had burned up. It had to be rebuilt again.

I realized God had really heard our prayer to "stop the ship." We were not going to get out of Africa until everyone had broken through spiritually. And we would not survive without perseverance coupled with dependence on God. Beginning a five-day fast, I shared the next day with the team the battle we were in and invited them to join me in prayer for it.

During our time in Dakar, I heard by letter that Joy Dawson came through Lausanne to teach in the School of Evangelism. Judi told her about our situation in Africa and asked her to seek the Lord for any word of encouragement He might give about getting us back home quickly. Joy prayed and came to Judi later, saying, "The Lord has shown me that the delays and challenges in Africa are the making of a leader." Then, instead of praying for me in Africa, Joy prayed for grace upon Judi carrying our second child and upon Lisa, who was missing her daddy so much.

Three days later Marc was flown back to Switzerland, where his father, a Swiss medical doctor, would oversee his convalescence.

On May 6, now over four months since we left Lausanne, André, Marie Christine, and I spent several hours ministering to one of our students. She told us she had once been involved in the occult. "I have this hazy, distant memory of me as a toddler lying in my crib. The face of my grandmother looked intently into my eyes. Shortly afterwards she died. I learned later she was a spiritist medium. In my teens I discovered I had an unnatural ability to do things I could not explain rationally. I realized she had transferred to me her demonic powers before her death." God graciously met us during the four hours we prayed for her and brought His freedom from this bondage. Nearly all of our students were now spiritually "on board the ship."

That same day, with shouts of "Hallelujah," we found a buyer and completed the legal papers for the sale of the white van. We were half way there. But according to my calculations, we were nearing the point of no return, where even if we sold both vans, we would not have enough for the plane tickets because of the additional amount we were spending on food and housing.

Two days later, for the team's rest day, a couple we met at one of the Dakar churches took us to a beach one and a half hours away. The setting was magnificent. Palm trees and beautiful white sand gently sloped into a gorgeous blue ocean. It was the heat of the day, and everyone dashed into the water to swim. We so enjoyed the cool water that we didn't notice a current slowly pulling us out to sea. Suddenly I heard one of our students screaming and waving her arms. Several of us swam to her. "Help me!" she gasped. "I'm exhausted. I can't keep swimming."

Though I'm not a strong swimmer, I swam alongside, assuring her we would make it to shore if she relaxed. I tried to pull her along, careful not to let her drag me under. But in a short time I also was exhausted. I began to fear that I couldn't make it back in. *Lord, please don't let us drown*, I pleaded in silent petition. Then I saw it. A large, flat rock jutting just above the surface of the water, covered in what looked like green moss. It disappeared when a wave swept onto it but reappeared when the wave passed over. If we could climb on top of that rock, I thought, we could catch our breath and eventually make it the rest of the way in.

I swam with all the strength I could muster and pulled us up on the rock. There was only room for two of us, so the others hung back. I clung to the rock as each wave that rolled in tried to pound us off. After two or three waves swept over us, I could no longer hold on. The next wave tore us off the rock and bashed us against several other rocks before washing us ashore. We struggled onto the beach with the help of several of our team. Our hands and legs were bleeding from multiple coral cuts, but we both were so thankful to be alive that we hardly noticed.

After assuring myself about the student's condition, I thought, *God, this was the last person needing to break through. The enemy tried to snatch her away, but now she's pulling with us. I believe all of the people You have given me are now spiritually "on board the ship." Please work the miracles we need for us to depart from Africa.*

The next morning a potential buyer came for the blue van. His offer was too low, so we refused it. In the early evening he returned, still unwilling to raise his offer. A second buyer arrived. So the first man, wanting to keep his place, immediately raised his bid. Then a third buyer came. That did it. The first man raised his offer again, and we struck a deal.

We went to the customs office the next day to register the sale, only to discover the buyer had backed down and torn up the papers. We called our students to prayer as I immediately went to find the second person who had shown a strong interest the day before. God answered our prayers, and the van sold. We went to the travel agency and purchased the available seats for most of the team on the next day's flight. I planned for André to lead the team on that flight. I would take a flight a couple of days later with the remaining students. But that evening André and the team insisted I go on the first flight. "Your family needs you," he said. "And besides, our team is doing okay. We're all on the ship now." He smiled and hugged me. I intended to refuse his kind offer, but then sensed the Lord assuring me it would be all right. André could wrap things up.

Sunday morning, May 11, we boarded our plane for Switzerland. It still seemed like a dream that in a few hours I would be back with my family, whom I missed so much. Judi was ready to deliver our second child, and I wondered if it would be a boy or a girl.

As we soared over North Africa, I sobered while reflecting on the past four and a half months. The many battles we had fought and how God had protected and delivered us flooded my mind. What a huge responsibility it was to be a spiritual leader. When God gives us responsibility to lead His people, He puts His awesome power into operation to bring to pass what He has called us to do. Regardless of the challenges we face, He wants us to work through them in unity. Disunity leads to lack of blessing and loss of spiritual protection. It leaves holes in our spiritual armor and opens us to the enemy's attacks. God had shown me and our team that he takes unity very seriously. We needed each other. With unity is blessing; without it is disaster.

When the flight attendant came by, offering a continental breakfast, I became conscious of the fact I was transitioning from an African lifestyle to a European one. I wondered what other adjustments I would need to make after so long in Africa. We had overcome so many challenges to obey God in this pioneering mission to French West Africa. I felt unbelievable fulfillment in ministering on this continent after so many years of anticipation. I was especially glad to have worked with Pastor Jean Glao in Abidjan, Ivory Coast. His enthusiasm and commitment to the Lord encouraged all of us, and I knew God used us to encourage him too. I hoped that I would be able to work with him again. There was so much need in West Africa—and so many potential opportunities for permanent YWAM workers in the region. *What future plans does God have for YWAM in French West Africa?* I wondered.

FIFTEEN

Multiplication and Relinquishment

JUDI and Lisa met us at the airport in Geneva. They each were so full of life. Judi looked ready to have our baby at any moment, and two-year-old Lisa was extremely talkative. I wondered how I looked to them, so weary from my travels and responsibilities.

That evening I fought an internal struggle as I sat across from them at the dinner table. It wasn't the food; French cuisine was an enjoyable change. But for the past four and a half months I had lived, thought, dreamed, and ministered in French. My mind screamed, *Use French.* It felt the most natural. But my relationship with Judi and Lisa had always been in English, and I needed to actively reconnect with them after such a long separation. Once I made that decision I was surprised at how quickly my inner world switched. All my quiet musings, my dreams, and my personal meditations with the Lord ceased to function in French. English became natural again.

Five weeks later our second child, Joseph Michael, was born a month overdue. He was a healthy, good-natured baby with soft blond hair and light brown eyes. Although Judi had struggled with the delayed birth, God had given us time as a family of three to get readjusted before adding our fourth member. Judi now understandably needed to focus more of her attention on the children and less on French Ministries, and I missed her involvement. I needed to refocus on French Ministries in Europe, since I had been so focused on pioneering our first ministry effort in French West Africa.

In July 1975, YWAM Europe began their summer ministry teams with a combined two-week training time in Holland. Over 370 young people representing thirty-two nations gathered; more than one hundred were assigned to work with us in French Europe. We divided these young people into ten teams that went to work in Belgium, Luxembourg, France (including Corsica), and Switzerland. I asked Tom and Cynthia Bloomer, who had been assisting me in French Ministries for two years, to take responsibility for the teams in Belgium and Luxembourg. I visited the teams in France and Switzerland. These were the first teams we had ever sent to Luxembourg and the island of Corsica. A team of Egyptian Christians came to witness to the North Africans in Marseille, France.

At the conclusion of the summer outreach, the ten French teams gathered in Lausanne for two days of reporting the summer's events. I heard stories about how God provided for their needs, opened many doors for evangelism, and birthed people into the kingdom. The team of sixteen Egyptian young people spoke with excitement about their experiences witnessing for Christ among the many North Africans in Marseille. Many told how God helped them overcome fears of witnessing, since it was forbidden in Egypt. In Marseille, many listened to their message. Other teams worked through the challenges of ministry and team life and saw people respond to the Lord. Christian youth groups and churches were strengthened through the influence of these teams.

It was exciting to see that the ministry foundations we had been slowly laying over the past several years had become solid. YWAM in French Europe was being accepted by the churches. They were open to collaborating and sending us their young people. The ministry was emerging.

That weekend Loren and Darlene Cunningham came through Lausanne. Judi and I invited them to our apartment for supper so I could give a report and show the slides of our Africa trip. After showing them our travel route and telling them numerous stories about what we had experienced and what I saw as the potential for ministry, I explained that several pastors and missionaries had asked us to consider returning on a permanent basis. Loren asked me about each place that had invited us back: what would be the ministry opportunities? Then he asked me which location I felt had the best options. My immediate response was "Abidjan, Ivory Coast."

The following week in early September, at a YWAM staff conference in England, I spoke to Loren again. As we stood in a brightly lit chapel, he queried, "Have you understood the significance of what you told me last week in your apartment about possible ministry opportunities in Africa?"

"Uh, no," I replied blankly.

"When Darlene and I returned to our room, we spoke about our time with you. We saw that God was in the process of calling you, of showing you His vision. Are you ready to pray and see what God is asking you in regard to Africa, the work there, and the timing of when to begin?"

My thoughts began to spin. I didn't have a quick answer for him, but I nervously said, "Okay," and slowly walked back to my room. The impact of what I heard began sinking into my spirit. Could this be the fulfillment of my lifelong dream to be a missionary in Africa?

Back home the following week, I needed to get some understanding about this Africa question. I went for a walk in the forest. The familiar path across the road led to where I often went when I needed to be alone with God. Walking between tall pine trees, I thought of the growing ministry being established in French-speaking Europe. A thought came to me that French Ministries in Europe was like a spiritual garden that had been planted and watered. The seeds had germinated. Everywhere young green sprouts were about to break through the hard ground. I knew intuitively that when the French expression of Youth With A Mission sprouted above the surface, the enemy's "winds of adversity" would try to blow it over. But it would be too late to stop what was happening, because strong, effective ministry had begun.

It was encouraging to see how ministry in French Europe had taken shape. But how did my life fit into the plan for Africa? Could I be involved in ministry on two continents? I opened my Bible and began to read Acts 13, my next daily reading. When I got to verses 44–52, I caught my breath. The words came alive. After Paul and Barnabas had preached to the Jews, God said to them, "I have made you a light for the Gentiles, that you may bring salvation to the ends of the earth" (v. 47). Was now the time to consider moving to French West Africa? Was I to seriously consider leading this involvement there? What would be the implications for the work in Europe? How could I leave this work I had birthed? I knew I had to be careful not to put the ministry in Europe at risk while trying to begin something new elsewhere.

I sat down on a log and breathed in the heavily oxygenated air. "Lord, if I am to be the one to begin YWAM in French West Africa, who is to take over responsibility in French Europe?" As soon as I asked, Tom Bloomer's name came to mind. Because Tom and I had been working together in French Ministries for two years, he had a very good grasp of things.

I began walking back. The air smelled fresh. Sunlight glowed above the thick foliage of tall trees as I descended the path that led to the road by my apartment.

Then other thoughts entered my mind. If I moved to French West Africa, I wouldn't have the personal satisfaction of seeing YWAM French Ministries in Europe finally emerge. I loved working in France and Switzerland. I had fallen in love with these people. And the time seemed so close when the work would produce a harvest of workers. Couldn't I enjoy that victory a little while? I also wondered if people would think ill of me for leaving. But if God was saying I had done my part in establishing YWAM in French Europe and He had another work for me to pioneer, who was I to say differently?

Over the weeks, I continued to seek God's direction, sometimes alone and sometimes with Judi (I was beginning to learn the importance of talking and praying with her about decisions that would greatly affect both of us). It became clearer I was to move. And Abidjan, Ivory

Coast, emerged as the probable location. I spent time in prayer with Don Stephens, who was now YWAM's director for Europe, the Middle East, and Africa, and with the other leaders at our YWAM center in Lausanne. God led me to Isaiah 54:2, "Enlarge the place of your tent, stretch your tent curtains wide, do not hold back; lengthen your cords, strengthen your stakes."

The joint conclusion of these leaders and me was that I was to lead a small, permanent team to French West Africa. Leaving in January, I would take the next French School of Evangelism along with my permanent team overland through the Sahara to Abidjan. When the students flew back to Europe after their three months, our small team would begin YWAM's first permanent ministry in French-speaking Africa. I asked Tom and Cynthia Bloomer to take over French Ministries in Europe in January, and they agreed. They would not be alone. About twenty full-time YWAM missionaries, many of whom were European, now worked in French Ministries.

Judi and I talked about the details of moving our family to Africa. Because our son was six months old, too young to make the overland trip, we decided that she and the kids would fly down to join me once our team arrived in Abidjan, Ivory Coast. Judi had seen the slides from our trip and had heard the stories, so she had an idea of the conditions in West Africa. We discussed the potential difficulties, but before actually experiencing things as a family, it was difficult to know what all the challenges would be.

The question I had on the plane ride from Senegal to Switzerland the previous year was now being answered: YWAM's future in French West Africa was coming into focus.

SIXTEEN

Ministry in Ivory Coast

JANUARY 2, 1976, dawned cold and rainy in Lausanne. Our nineteen-member team of fifteen students and four long-term team members was preparing to depart for the second trip across the Sahara to West Africa. We would travel in four Volkswagen vans and one Land Rover and be joined again on our long journey by students and staff from the school in Germany.

Crossing the border into Morocco, our group discovered that war had just broken out between Morocco and Algeria over Morocco's annexing Spanish Sahara. Two days later, across the country at the eastern border, we were denied entry into Algeria, being told that the crossing was closed because of the war. We learned we might get through to West Africa from southern Morocco, via Spanish Sahara, by Moroccan military escort to Mauritania and then to Senegal. But when we traveled south to request permission to make this passage, we learned that Algerian rebels had attacked a recent convoy, killing all the passengers in a European tourist vehicle.

We turned to the Lord, inquiring what to do. We realized that He had not sent us south; we had made that decision on our own. Asking the Lord's forgiveness for not consulting Him, we headed back to the Morocco–Algeria border.

Early the next morning we began the border crossing procedures a second time. First we checked out of Morocco: each passport was stamped with an exit stamp, each person turned in his or her currency exchange forms to prove no money had been exchanged on the black market, and each vehicle's *Carnet de Passage* was processed for exiting the country. After several hours we crossed the quarter-mile stretch of no man's land to the Algerian border post. Once there, we were again refused entrance into Algeria. The border official was unusually hostile to us, yelling that they were at war and how dare we try to come through. Driving back to the Moroccan border post, we did in reverse all the paperwork we had just completed. That night we prayed that God would open the border for us.

The next day we again spent several hours checking out of Morocco and going across to Algeria, only to be refused entrance by the same angry man. Checking back into Morocco with all the paperwork took the rest of the day. Again that night we prayed.

The following morning, to avoid the hours of paperwork for everyone to check out of Morocco, I checked out personally and walked across the no man's land with our thirty-nine passports to Algeria. The air was hot, and flies buzzed around my face. I was refused by the same irate official. The next day I did the same thing with the same results. That evening we cried to the Lord for His direction. We sensed we should drive our vehicles and take all our people across the border one more time and believe God to open the way.

Early the following morning, January 18, we checked out of Morocco and drove across no man's land. Arriving at the Algerian border post, we met a new official who did not turn us away. For several hours the inspectors searched every vehicle and every suitcase. At one point an inspector found a lump in the lining of my van. Instantly guards came from everywhere. A sharp knife sliced open the lining, and a wad of wrapped paper fell out. With a sneer the inspector began unwrapping what he likely thought was a stash of drugs. Having no idea what it was, I held my breath as each layer was peeled away. When the final layer was opened, there was nothing inside. The wad of paper had only been a spacer to keep the van's lining from buckling. Laughing with embarrassment, the official waved us through. We quickly loaded our suitcases and departed before he could change his mind. We drove into Algeria rejoicing that God had opened the way.

When we arrived at the oasis of In Salah, we set up camp in a thicket of palm trees. An old, bearded French desert dweller struck up a conversation. "How many are in your group?" he asked.

"We're thirty-nine people," I responded.

He looked astonished. "Are you the infamous thirty-nine who spent a week trying to cross the border? Are you the one who walked the passports across the no man's land several times?"

"Yes, we are. And, yes, I am," I assured him. "How did you hear about that?"

"I have a friend at the border post who told me the story." He explained that the first official hated Americans, because America had sided with Morocco regarding Spanish Sahara. Every time the official saw my American passport on top of the passports, he cursed in Arabic, saying my passport had soiled the rest like human excrement. But that Sunday he had been called away and a new official filled in for him.

After that trying delay at the border, our travels went more smoothly. On March 4, two long and busy months after departing from Lausanne, we arrived in Abidjan, rejoicing in the Lord's faithfulness in bringing us back to this place. This time crossing the desert we had great team unity, didn't get lost in the desert, and didn't see a single African killer bee. We felt that during our last trip we had broken through the enemy's attacks and defeated his attempts to keep us out of Africa.

A week later Judi and our children, three-year-old Lisa and eight-month-old Joey, as well as André Sivager flew down from Switzerland to join us. As I stood watching them disembark the airplane, I absent-mindedly pulled at my sticky shirt to break its cling on my body. My kids were startled by the bushy black beard I had grown during the past two months. In the middle of my family's first night with me, I woke to

Judi's screams. "A huge cockroach! It's crawling on you, Joe," she yelled. Within a few minutes I found and killed it. Tranquility reigned once again.

The students spent almost the entire month with André in the interior of Ivory Coast, ministering in churches, youth meetings, and open-air rallies. They returned to Abidjan in time to sing and testify on television on April 1. The next day they flew back to Switzerland. The vehicles remained with us for future teams from Lausanne.

I rented two empty, unfinished houses in the small fishing village of M'Pouto to accommodate our permanent team made up of three single guys (Charles, Hubert, and André) and two single girls (Esther and Marie-Christine) plus my family. André was from France, and the other four were Swiss. In Luke 10:5–6 Jesus told His disciples that when they entered a town or village, they should search for a "man of peace" to assist in the provision of their lodging and ministry. We were blessed with two men of peace, Swiss missionary Charles-Daniel, who helped us find housing, and Pastor Jean Glao, who opened doors for our ministry.

I took Judi and our children to see the houses before we moved in. Driving through several miles of bush on a dusty dirt track, we came out along a brackish lagoon where a man in a small dugout canoe fished about fifty yards offshore. We slowed as villagers walked along the road, many of them women wearing beautiful head wraps made of the same material as their colorful dresses. About fifteen houses circled a sandy area forming the center of our newly adopted village. At the far end, at the lagoon's shimmering shoreline, sat several more dugout canoes. I was told M'Pouto had about two hundred inhabitants, including a group of Bambara people (formerly from Mali) led by a man they called Le Vieux (the Old One).

Though I had only stopped for a few seconds, a group of about twenty barefoot children gathered and began chanting, "*Gan gan, tou-babou. Gan gan, toubabou.*" I learned later those words meant "white man" in the local Ebrié language and in Dioula, a regional trade language.

Just beyond the village, our two houses sat on either side of the track. I stopped in front of a two-story cinder-block house to our left.

The hollow shell had an unfinished interior and a flat cement slab roof with rebar sticking up for an additional floor. The windows gaped at us, trying to hide all the work that awaited us inside.

"Look, Judi, that's where we'll house the guys and hold our first school!" My enthusiasm wasn't impressing Judi. "I know it's a mess right now, but it'll look like a mission training school sooner than you think."

"There's a lot of work to be done before that," she remarked.

Without responding, I continued to pour out my vision. "There's enough land around the house to plant a garden to keep costs down and train more African students. But enough of that for now. Lisa, look! That's where we're going to live. Come on, I'll show you."

I pulled forward another ten yards and parked on the right side of the dirt track in front of a one-story, tin-roofed house. I grabbed Joey out of the car and escorted Lisa over the sandy strip in front. We skirted around a palm tree that neighbors had cut down to make palm whiskey. "Don't worry, Lisa, we'll plant grass, and in no time you'll have a nice place to play."

On our right a little room, intended as the outdoor kitchen, now was full of building supplies. In my excitement I led my family inside the house, ignoring Judi's silence. I swung my arm in an expansive semi-circle, exclaiming, "Look how large this front room is, Judi. This will be an excellent place for our team meetings as well as our meal times. If we put benches around the walls, we can hold classes and public services here until we finish fixing up the two-story house." Next we viewed the three bedrooms down the hall: one for the girls, one temporarily for the guys, and one for our family. A simple bathroom with no running water lay to the right.

Judi rode in silence on our way back to town. We both knew this would be hard, but I hoped it wouldn't be that hard. Because the houses were not habitable, our team found temporary lodging at a missionary guesthouse in Cocody, a suburb of Abidjan.

One day while at Cocody, Joey began experiencing strong abdominal pain, and we rushed him to the hospital. While he was being examined, an African couple brought in a two-year-old girl. She had been treated by a village witch doctor. On her body and around her mouth were the remains of various powdery potions. The next day we returned to the hospital for a follow-up visit and asked the doctor about the little girl. He told us she had died in the night, explaining that frequently children were brought to the hospital only after the village witch doctor had tried all his spells. Many were so weak when they arrived that they often died. With deep sadness we redoubled our prayers for these precious people who desperately needed God. Joey recovered quickly, but so many children suffered needlessly.

Life in Ivory Coast, we were learning more every day, was very different from life in Switzerland and other parts of the world that my family had experienced. One difference that we struggled with was the climate of Ivory Coast, which is located near the equator. We were soaked in sweat the moment we stepped outside into the subtropical heat. Judi had never experienced such brutal humidity. God must have heard Judi's prayers for relief, because Charles-Daniel and his wife invited our team to move into their four-bedroom apartment while they were on a trip out of the country. Located in the village of Anono, it was just two miles from M'Pouto, thus shortening our daily commute to work on the house. Their apartment had purified water and bedrooms with air conditioning, a true blessing in the almost unbearable heat and humidity of the rainy season.

Our single-story house was nearing completion, though the walls needed paint and the electricity needed connecting. The house had no running water, but it did have a bucket-flushed toilet that was connected to a homemade septic tank. For our shower, a bucket with a sprinkling-can head attached at the bottom hung in the bathroom. Pulling a string released water for a quick, cold shower. The rooms, lacking ceilings, were open all the way to the roof's tin underside. When it rained, which was often and intense in that season, the sound of the downpour drowned out any conversation below. During the day, the sun beat down on the roof and created a sauna effect.

Charles, one of our Swiss team members, could fix or build anything, and his creativity was a huge blessing as we worked to improve the houses. Concentrating our efforts on the single-story house, we began installing ceilings. Then we designed beds for everyone, making mattresses from pieces of foam we had used when traveling across the

Sahara. We installed mosquito nets above every bed. Finally, we bought a used refrigerator and propane stove from an expatriate family moving back to Europe. Within a month the place was more or less livable.

On a hot, sunny day in the last week of April, our family loaded our suitcases into the Land Rover, said good-bye to that much-appreciated apartment, and moved with the team into the single-story house. Sweat trickled down my face and dripped down my back as we carried boxes and baskets inside and began setting up. The house had no curtains, glass windows, or screens, only wooden shutters that let in malaria-carrying mosquitoes. We used wooden crates for furniture. Benches sat around a plank picnic table. Judi seemed to be in shock as we moved our two children from the beautifully decorated, air-conditioned apartment into this semifinished cement-floored structure with no running water and inadequate light to read by at night. "I can't write our parents about these conditions," she mumbled. "They'll worry. But we'll make the best of it."

With the help of our capable team members, we were moved in by the end of the day. I was so grateful for their help. And in spite of the living conditions, it felt good to finally be settled in Africa, the land that had fascinated me so much as a child. This was the fulfillment of my nineteen-year dream, and it was exciting to begin learning about the local culture and way of life. But this wasn't without its challenges.

Judi worked hard to build a nest for our family. Instead of having silverware, she made do with plastic camping utensils and equipment. Shopping for fruit and vegetables at the local outdoor market required much haggling for prices. The locally grown fruit and vegetables had to be soaked in a potassium permanganate solution for twenty minutes to kill as many germs and amoebas as possible.

André proved to be a talented procurer of food, while Esther, a Swiss team member and an excellent cook, created amazing dishes with just a few ingredients. On Sunday mornings, after sifting weevils out of the flour, she prepared a Swiss traditional braided sweet bread called *tresse*. We also learned to prepare a local starch (called *adtieké* in Ebrié) by grinding manioc root and pressing out the white, sticky liquid. Once fried, it looked like rice, though its agreeable taste carried no resemblance to it.

To sleep at night, for security reasons we closed the shutters on our house, which completely blocked all airflow. When we rolled over in bed under our unmoving mosquito nets, our sheets stuck and pulled out as we dragged them with us.

One night we experienced an alarming part of the culture we had entered. After putting the children in their beds and covering the beds with their mosquito nets, Judi and I heard the sound of drums and people dancing in the village. Within a few seconds I felt the force of a demonic presence hit the side of our home. When it hit, I felt an almost palpable shaking, and the children immediately began screaming. Quickly running to them, I took authority over the powers of darkness and bound them in Jesus' name. Then the children settled down. This happened for several nights, until I began to pray over the children before putting them to bed. Binding the enemy, I asked the Lord to put angels around them. When I prayed this in faith, Lisa and Joey would sleep through the night. If I prayed just out of habit, they would wake up screaming. I soon learned to mean what I prayed. Spiritual warfare became a way of life in those days.

Each morning Lisa went out to play with the village children. She learned to eat green mangos and kill vipers. One day the village women invited her to go with them to fetch river water. Lisa followed them for a mile with her small plastic basin and returned proudly carrying it on her head filled with water like the rest of the women.

To make water available at home, we hired a villager to dig a surface well. He didn't look very healthy; the whites of his eyes were a sallow yellow color. But he was the person the villagers recommended as the well digger. He sat on the sandy ground where we wanted the well and began filling a bucket. A small boy assisted him by emptying the bucket and returning it to be refilled. In a couple of days he hit water at just over six feet deep. He sat in the water and deepened the well to enable us to have a good volume of water.

While the well was being dug, I built a twenty-foot water tower to hold a fifty-five gallon drum, planning to eventually pump water from the well into the barrel. From there pipes would run to the kitchen and bathroom. But there was much work to do before we installed pipes and had well water available inside the house. In the meantime we still had to drive five miles roundtrip to fetch our daily supply of purified drinking water in a multitude of clear plastic containers.

Three weeks after moving to M'Pouto, as I drove through the village, I listened for the by-now familiar chant of the children running behind us. Instead of "*Gan gan, toubabou,*" I heard them chanting, "Lisa, Lisa, Lisa." It struck me that we had stopped being foreigners. We were now the parents of Lisa, and the children wanted her to come out to play. Lisa, in her childish simplicity and openness, had won a way into their hearts, and that opened a door to the village for us. I realized that our children are part of God's plan as we reach out to others. He uses whole families in missions, not just parents.

The men in the village had two, three, or as many as six wives. This shocked me at first, but I realized that many of these people just had marriage problems multiplied several times over. In spite of cultural differences, these were people in need of healing and restoration. In my walks through the village I also noticed an African albino teenager. I saw what looked like longing in his eyes. My heart went out to him, but he usually avoided me. Nevertheless, many of the people our team encountered responded to friendship and Christian love as we reached out in humility. After visiting at someone's home, before leaving we had to ask them for "the road." Departing came only when they granted us "the road." And this didn't always come immediately.

Our team's focus was not just on the people in M'Pouto. We organized summer camps as well as training and evangelism outreaches. Speaking engagements at various churches and youth groups had begun to open up to us. We also wanted to start an affordable training school to prepare young people for involvement in missions.

As our ministry was progressing, I began to think of the upcoming 1976 Summer Olympic Games outreach in Montreal, Canada. The year before, while I was still director of YWAM's French Ministries in Europe, I had agreed to recruit one hundred French young people to go to this event. Though this was no longer my responsibility, deep down I still had a desire to go to the outreach. *Is this only a desire to finish up a previous commitment, or is it to represent people coming from French West Africa?* I wondered. *How can I possibly go when there is so much to do in M'Pouto and the surrounding area?*

But the more I thought about it, the more I felt I was to leave Africa for a brief time to go to the outreach in Montreal. And since the outreach was in North America and our family hadn't been back there in two years, Judi and I planned to take the children to see our parents on the way. That way our parents could meet their new grandson for the first time. Judi and I also planned to purchase items we couldn't find at the markets in West Africa. The biggest things on my list were a roll of screening to mosquito-proof the house with and a water pump for our well.

Just a few days before our plane was to depart, we scheduled our first official meeting with the village chief. I knew that learning the proper protocol was important within this culture. I went with André Sivager, because he would be in charge of the team in my absence. We were not to look at or talk directly to the chief. We worked through a third party, one of our neighbors. The meeting went very well, and the chief offered to present us personally to various groups in the village. He would arrange three meetings, and everyone invited was expected to be present. André would coordinate our team's involvement and speaking at these gatherings.

On the day of our departure, the whole team took us to the airport. Praying over André and the team, I entrusted them into God's hands during my family's short absence. Stopping through Switzerland, we packed our household belongings into twelve barrels for shipment to Ivory Coast. We were fully committed to Africa now. I relaxed as we flew to the United States, confident that we would be back in M'Pouto by the end of the summer.

SEVENTEEN

Stopped and Redirected

ON OUR flight from New York to San Jose, California, on June 14, 1976, I became violently ill. I had taken malaria preventative pills while in Africa, so I was dismayed by what seemed to be a malaria attack. A flight attendant moved me to the first class compartment where I could lie down and the sound of my relentless retching would disturb fewer passengers. My family remained in the economy section, but Judi was allowed to come up to see how I was doing periodically. When my condition worsened, the flight attendant returned and said, "The pilot will make an emergency landing in Denver, Colorado, where an ambulance will take you to the hospital. Then we will continue our flight to California." Judi and I both protested, assuring them that I had malaria, which was only spread by mosquitoes and would not infect the other passengers. I told the attendant that I had medication in my checked baggage that I could take once we got to San Jose. So the pilot continued the flight.

It had been two years since I had said good-bye to my parents and my brother and sisters. I was so eager to see them, but when we arrived in San Jose, I could barely walk.

My family greeted us warmly. After taking a strong dose of malaria medication, I went off for a good night's sleep. I felt so much better the next day that I didn't give that attack of sickness another thought. We focused on family and on plans for the Olympics outreach in Montreal. I also packed and shipped to Africa a box of hand tools, household items, and birthday candles for our children.

During the Fourth of July bicentennial weekend, the celebration of the United States' two hundredth birthday, I became violently ill again. I had an extremely high fever and couldn't keep anything down, not even water. I lay in bed, thirsty, dry, and delirious. I hallucinated, seeing strange images floating around me. After several days, with my condition deteriorating, my family took me to the hospital.

I lay in the emergency room not quite sure what was going on, except that I desperately wanted to stop the dry heaves and ease my overpowering thirst. When a doctor appeared, my muddled mind struggled to follow his questions and give an answer. "I have just returned from West Africa, where I have been working as a missionary. I thought this might be malaria, so I took a strong dose of malaria medication, but it hasn't helped. Please, I'm so thirsty. Is there anything you can give me to help me hold some water down?" He gave me a shot that stopped my retching, then asked a nurse to give me a small cup of crushed ice. It felt almost heavenly to hold that ice in my mouth and finally begin to absorb some liquid into my fever-ravaged system. The doctor smiled. "I'm a Christian, and I prayed this morning for the Lord to give me an interesting case. You are the answer to my prayer."

After a series of blood tests, the doctor admitted me to the hospital. He ordered an IV to rehydrate me and then performed a spinal tap to test for spinal meningitis. When the doctor returned later in the day, I noticed a new seriousness in his demeanor. "You have infectious hepatitis. A very strong strain," he said. "The hepatitis virus we have here in the States has a lower liver count; yours is extremely high." Then he asked to speak to Judi. When he found she was gone, he left. I was glad because I was exhausted and wanted to sleep.

The next morning Judi came to visit. She and my mother had contacted churches and friends to pray. A friend explained my need at a spiritual leadership conference in her church that evening. One of the speakers, Jean Darnall, sensed this need was urgent and invited the people to pray for me. They persisted in prayer until they sensed the burden lift, as if God had said, "I have heard your prayers." And God had. Within two days my fever dropped and my liver count fell to half its elevated intensity, so the doctor released me from the hospital. I returned to my parent's home for bed rest. When Judi canceled our trip to Montreal, I was too exhausted to argue.

I returned to the doctor's office for weekly blood tests, which showed rapid improvement. On the first visit the doctor sat me down to talk. "Joe, I recommend that you don't ever return to Africa."

"But I have to return," I protested. "I have a team waiting for me."

"Well, okay, if you feel you have to return, I strongly recommend that you wait for at least one year. If you have a relapse within the first year, you will probably continue to have relapses the rest of your life. If, however, you get through this first year, there's a good chance you'll never have a relapse. The intense climate and living conditions in Africa will produce further loss of your health, not restoration of it," he explained.

"My team is waiting for me in Africa. I have to get back to them," I said.

Seeing my strong resistance, he continued to reason with me. "When I admitted you to the hospital, I was very concerned by your condition. Do you remember when I came to your hospital room that first day and asked for your wife? I wanted to prepare her for the worst. Your liver was so badly damaged I thought it would stop functioning. I didn't think you would live through that first night. Yes, God did answer prayer, but don't do anything foolish."

Because I had not liked either of the choices the doctor gave me—never returning to Africa or waiting one year to return—I decided to ignore them and not tell anyone about what he said. I left that subject in God's hands.

I was still exhausted and could barely spend a couple of hours a day out of bed, but in the days ahead I grew determined to return to

M'Pouto. At the end of August, YWAM was having a leadership conference in Wisconsin. Since it was on our way, I thought we could stop for
the one-week event on our trip back to Africa. I booked our plane tickets for Africa via Wisconsin and decided not to give the doctor's advice
any further thought. I hoped that in Wisconsin I would receive a miraculous healing so that I could regain the strength needed for our return
to Africa. As Judi and I packed our suitcases, I made sure to include a
small water pump to move our well water in M'Pouto up to the fifty-
five gallon drum on our water tower.

We flew from San Jose to Kansas City to visit Judi's folks. During our
time there Judi had a miscarriage. As a result, both of us were exhausted
physically and emotionally when we arrived at the conference facilities
in Eagle River, Wisconsin, on August 23.

One of the first things I did before the conference started was to
arrange a meeting with Don Stephens, who was the YWAM regional
director for Europe, the Middle East, and Africa; and Loren Cunningham, who had moved from Switzerland to Hawaii, pioneering a training center that would eventually become the University of the Nations.

On a Tuesday afternoon in a small, private sitting room overlooking the lake, Judi and I met with Don and Loren. We sat comfortably in
large overstuffed chairs. I shared the events of the past several months,
from our time at M'Pouto to the present. "What I really need is a miracle from God. I need a full restoration of health to have the strength to
return to Africa," I concluded.

"What did your doctor say to you about returning to Africa?" Loren
asked.

"Uh . . . well, um . . . actually what the doctor recommended was for
me not to return to Africa for at least a year, if ever," I stammered. "But
I'm not open to that." I avoided Judi's stunned stare. She hadn't heard
this before.

"Did the doctor explain why he recommended that?" Loren interjected in a gentle voice.

"Well . . . yes. He told me that with my weakened health it would be
easy for me to relapse under the adverse conditions in Africa. Having
a relapse of hepatitis in the first year would probably lead to regular
relapses. Without a relapse this year, I probably would never have one."

"What do you feel about that, Joe?" Loren asked in a kind, fatherly manner.

"That's why I'm here asking for prayer. I need God to heal me so that I won't have these complications. I realize I don't have the strength I need to go back. But I have a team waiting for me and a burning desire to fulfill my calling to Africa. I've waited twenty years for this time."

Don spoke up. "Joe, have you considered taking a year's sabbatical to regain your health before going back to Africa?"

"No, I haven't. What would become of my team in M'Pouto and all that we have already done to establish the work there?"

"From what your doctor said, you need to seriously think about it," Don responded.

"You would be welcome to come to Hawaii with your family and take a sabbatical year with us," Loren said. "You could work on a reduced schedule and take the time you need to rest and regain your health. It has been over two years since I moved from Europe. I would love to have you working with me again."

"I appreciate your concern and your offer, but what about my team in M'Pouto? We are just beginning. That's where I belong."

Don broke in again. "Joe, I believe you need to seriously pray about Loren's offer. Yes, there are some implications regarding what will happen to the work in Africa, but we can live with them. It would mean closing down your work in M'Pouto and having the team return to Switzerland. But there are other people in YWAM whose works have been closed for various reasons, and people have not thought ill of them. This could be the Lord wanting to give you time to recuperate."

By this time my throat had tightened and tears coursed down my cheeks. I fumbled for my handkerchief while I tried to compose myself. My throat kept squeezing tighter, and I inhaled forcefully, trying to catch my breath. Feeling the anguish of disappointment, I couldn't hold the sobs back any longer. I wasn't worried about whether people would think ill of me; I just wanted my strength back so I could get back to Africa to fulfill my lifelong dream.

It seemed forever before I was able to regain my composure. Don and Loren both prayed for me and encouraged me to pray over the next few days about what my next step should be. Though I didn't want to, I assured them I would. But closing the work and having the team return to Switzerland was not at all what I wanted.

When Judi and I returned to our room, she was furious. "What were you thinking? Why didn't you tell me what the doctor told you?" she blurted out.

I stammered and finally said, "I concluded we couldn't do what he said; we have a team waiting for us in Africa. So I decided not to muddy the waters. But I'm sorry. I should have told you. Will you forgive me?"

Judi was always quick to pardon. "Yes, Joe, I forgive you."

"Judi, I'm not ready to pray about Hawaii yet. Let's give it a little time."

I decided to write a letter to André and the team in M'Pouto to update them about my health and gently prepare them for things that might develop not exactly as planned. But since I still didn't know what I was going to do, I didn't draw any conclusions in the letter.

A couple of days later, when I was finally ready to hear what God might say, I asked Judi to join me to pray about our next step. I told the Lord that I was willing to do whatever. As I prayed, I had a deep sense in my spirit that God was directing us to Hawaii. Judi had the same conviction. I asked the Lord to confirm that conviction, and the thought came to my mind to read Isaiah 49. In the New American Standard Bible it begins, "Listen to Me, O islands . . . ." I couldn't escape it any longer. I prayed out loud, "Okay, Lord, if that is what You want, I'll do it."

I told Don about my decision to go to Hawaii as well as my concern for my team waiting in Africa. We came to the conclusion, painful for me, that the team would return to Switzerland. Don would oversee that as the regional director. Tom Bloomer was informed of this, and he recommended to both of us that the team be allowed to remain at least until the next French School of Evangelism group from Lausanne came down to Africa. We both agreed to that glimmer of life and hope.

I wrote a second letter to the team, explaining what I would be doing. Then I called the airlines and canceled the rest of our flight and applied the balance to tickets for Kailua-Kona, Hawaii.

When the leadership conference ended, our family got on a plane again—heading in a totally different direction from what I had planned a week and a half earlier. It was now September, and my team had been expecting us back in Africa at the end of this month. In such a short time my whole world had turned upside down. We touched down in San Jose to repack at my parents' home. Then we were off to Hawaii.

When our plane took off, all I could think was that in spite of God's direction for Hawaii, I was going in the opposite direction from my heart and my calling.

EIGHTEEN

Learning God's Lessons

GLANCING out the plane's window, I saw a large island over the left wing in a vast ocean of turquoise blue water. Two high mountains stood majestically at the island's center, their land mass gently sloping down to the shore. Big billowy clouds shrouded each of these old volcanic summits. As we descended over fields of black lava rock, I had the eerie sensation that we were landing on the moon instead of Hawaii. I arrived in Kailua-Kona in body but not in heart. That was still in Africa.

The Lord had directed Loren and Darlene Cunningham and other YWAM leaders to come to Kona on Hawaii's Big Island, and they came in obedience. But the place was little more than a village at the time. Housing was scarce. YWAM had not yet obtained a permanent property. People lived in various houses and apartments all over town. On our second day there, a five-bedroom place opened up for us to share with four other families. Our family moved into one bedroom, and schedules were quickly established so the ten adults and eight children could wash each morning in one of the two bathrooms. Privacy was a thing of the past.

I worked at the pace my frail health would allow. One afternoon I was resting, after having spent the morning doing repairs in the house. I looked around our twelve-foot by twelve-foot room. Three of the aquamarine walls had bright yellow and orange fish painted at various levels. The fourth wall was covered with unpainted four-foot by eight-foot sheets of rough-hewn plywood. All the room lacked was a fishing net draped across the ceiling to give one the feeling of being a small fish trapped in an aquarium. I decided right then I would have to repaint the walls off-white to get us out of the "fish bowl."

Thanks to the hot Hawaiian sun, it felt like I was swimming in my own perspiration each time I went inside our room. That afternoon I tried to sleep but couldn't, so instead I grabbed a letter that I had just received from my team in M'Pouto. It said that André had departed for Europe to take a position as assistant pastor in France. Because I had not returned as scheduled, he had to turn the team over to another team member. The letter continued, "Joe, as you can imagine, we needed several days of reflection to make decisions with a fresh mind. . . . For the long-term work, you were the one with the vision. We have a heart for evangelism in the village, finishing up the two houses, and preparing the second house for a school, but we were waiting more than anything else for your return." Those last words hit me like a hammer.

I got up and paced around the room. In spite of my fatigue, I couldn't lie in bed with those frustrations in my heart. "Lord, why am I here? My team needs me there now, not next year. I was the one You gave the vision to for beginning the work in French West Africa. Wouldn't it be just as easy for me to lie in bed in Africa as in this Hawaiian heat? Can't I return there now?"

My prayer didn't get higher than the ceiling; the heavens were closed. I stormed out of my room and marched outside, but I found no relief. Why couldn't the Lord understand that I wanted to fulfill my childhood vision? I felt so alone here, thousands of miles away from my good friends. We had been through so much together already, and they needed me even more now.

Over the next several weeks, Judi and I repainted our room. More letters from Africa followed, and pressures built up. My not returning had shaken up the team. I had no answers as I fought between frustration and anger.

One afternoon I reached my breaking point. Marching into the living room, I tried to relax in a brown canvas chair, but I quickly got up and began pacing back and forth, feeling more hurt by the moment. Staring up at the dingy white ceiling, I thought, *Why did this have to happen, God? Why couldn't I still be in Africa with my team?*

As I paced, my spirit settled down. Sitting back in the armchair again, I prayed, *Lord, please help me understand what's happening.* In the quietness of that humid afternoon, I remembered something Joy Dawson taught at my School of Evangelism in Switzerland several years earlier. She spoke about the children of Israel being tested in the desert. God humbled and tried them to teach them about Himself (Deut. 8:3). Because they refused to submit to Him, they ended up going around those mountains many times instead of passing through the wilderness and out the other side to the Promised Land. Joy challenged us that if we didn't learn what God wanted to teach us, we would end up going around that "mountain" again. Because our learning God's lesson was so important to God, He would give us another opportunity at a later time to learn the same lesson in a more difficult circumstance.

As those implications settled on my spirit, I realized that I was in God's will in the middle of one of those desert times. In my stubbornness I was about to miss the lesson and end up going around this "mountain" again. "Lord," I blurted out, "I don't want to go through this again. If this time almost killed me, what will the next time be like? Please forgive me for being unwilling to submit to You. I accept Your will and yield to You. If You want me to be here in Hawaii now, that's okay with me. Please teach me everything you want me to learn, whatever the personal cost."

A stillness and peace began to settle over my spirit that had not been in my heart since I grudgingly came to Kona weeks before. I felt as light as a feather; my anger and frustrations slipped away. My heart was at peace.

After this, God immediately began teaching me things He wanted me to learn. The first thing was that He was my heavenly Father. I had known this in my head, but needed to know it in my heart. God wanted me to experience Him in my daily life. Now when I spent time alone with Him in prayer or reading my Bible, I sensed the closeness of His presence. This became a daily event during those weeks. Psalm 23:4 began to take on heart-meaning for me. "Even though I walk through the valley of the shadow of death, I will fear no evil, *for you are with me.*" God, my loving Father, was walking with me in the midst of the valley. I wasn't alone.

In the coming weeks our family began attending Mokuaikaua, the first church established in the Hawaiian Islands when missionaries arrived on April 4, 1820. Through the church, we connected with the local culture. We attended the quarterly *Hoike*, a gathering of the Sunday schools from the small Hawaiian churches in the surrounding towns and villages. This event always finished with a huge *lu'au* of authentic local foods, including some of my favorite dishes: *kalua* pig (cooked in an underground *imu*, or oven); chicken long rice; *lau lau* (steamed butterfish, beef, and pork wrapped in taro and ti leaves); *lomi lomi* salmon (cold diced salmon, tomatoes, and onions); *poi* (a thick paste of pounded taro); potato/mac salad; and *haupia* (coconut pudding dessert). As people got to know us at church potlucks, picnics, and Sunday-school classes, they eventually accepted us into their extended family. Our children called the women "Auntie" and the men "Uncle."

A thought began growing in my heart: *While I am here, why don't I take a team to visit French Polynesia and the other French-speaking islands of the South Pacific?* In early April 1977 in my daily Bible reading I came across Isaiah 18. As I read verses one and two, I caught my breath; they seemed to speak directly to me about that growing desire to go to French Polynesia. "Woe to the land of whirring wings along the rivers of Cush, which sends envoys by sea in papyrus boats over the water. Go, swift messengers, to a people tall and smooth-skinned, to a people feared far and wide, an aggressive nation of strange speech, whose land is divided by rivers."

I had heard that the islands of the South Pacific were first settled by early Polynesians from the Marquesas Islands, who came in double-hulled canoes. Some historians say that aggressive, feared Tahitian warriors came later and conquered the islands. Was God saying we should go as messengers to these people to bring His word?

I spoke to Loren about my idea. His wise response was that my first priority was to rebuild my health. If this was from God, He would provide a team at the right moment. And confirmation of God's timing would be a team coming together. I committed this to the Lord, waiting to see when He would release the team.

The next thing God began to teach me was that my trust in and commitment to Him had to be based on who He is, not on my circumstances. This understanding came as I read Daniel 3. Daniel's three friends were told by King Nebuchadnezzar that if they didn't bow down to his golden image, he would throw them into a fiery furnace. Their response was, "The God we serve is able to save us from it. . . . But *even if He does not* . . . we will not serve your gods or worship the image of gold you have set up" (vv. 17–18). Their commitment and trust in God was not based on their deliverance. They were willing to trust God, even if He didn't deliver. Could I trust God when it looked like He wouldn't deliver me from difficult circumstances? I wondered if I would have to learn this through a "fiery furnace" experience, but I couldn't imagine what that would look like.

Daniel's three friends had greater victory by going through the fiery furnace. If they had been saved from going in, their only victory would have been avoiding the furnace. But as a result of their going through it and trusting God in the midst of it, the king honored and praised their God. He decreed death to any who spoke against their God, for, he declared, no other god could save in this way (vv. 28–29). God, I realized, is always trustworthy and full of love and compassion. The enemy lies to us about God and accuses Him of wrongdoing. But we must refuse those lies.

Later that April, Don Stephens was in Kona for a planning meeting with other YWAM regional leaders. During one of their coffee breaks, I met with Loren and Don. We walked a short distance and sat on an old stone wall. Though I was still not able to put in a full day's work, I was slowly regaining my strength. I mentioned again my interest in exploring the mission needs in the French-speaking islands of the South

Pacific. They agreed that the French parts of the South Pacific needed the visit of a YWAM team. While the sun warmed the back of my neck, I listened as they talked enthusiastically about implications of YWAM's involvement in these places. Though our conversation lasted only a few minutes, it raised a question I had not considered. Was I supposed to be involved somehow in long-term ministry plans for the Pacific region?

A few days later I got alone with God to consider the implications of that conversation. By this time our family had moved into a two-bedroom apartment my heavenly Father had graciously provided. I slipped into my bedroom and knelt at the bed. "Lord, so many changes have taken place over the past two years that I'm not sure what You want for me anymore. I have a love for and a desire to work in several places of the French world, and yet some of this seems to be in question." Kneeling there, I had a growing sense God wanted me to give Him back the vision I had for the French regions of the world that were so dear to me. I held my hands out in front of me, opened upward, handing back to the Lord each precious gift and calling He had given me. I spoke slowly and deliberately, weighing each word. "Lord, I give You back my burden and calling for French Europe, French West Africa, and the French Pacific and Asia. These were Yours to start with. They came from You, and I return them to You." I moved my hands forward as if to put these places back into the Lord's hands.

A conviction swept over me that God had in fact taken them back. My spirit felt the void left as these dreams departed. A great sense of loss flooded my soul, expressing itself in physical pain. The nerves in my face twitched. Deep, uncontrollable sobs shook my body. I doubled over in pain and wept, letting my body and emotions express the grief I felt.

Finally, calmness enveloped me; I could pray again. "Each of these areas is totally Yours. I relinquish all my rights to them. But, Lord, are there any of those areas that You desire to return to me?" As I waited in silent trust before my precious heavenly Father, an astonishingly clear impression came to my mind: *Pacific and Asia.* Nothing more came to me. The impression had not specified the French areas. Then a question came to my mind, one that had an implied answer, but one I knew I had to ask. "After this summer, should I go back to Ivory Coast or commit myself here to pioneer into the Pacific and Asia?" The answer came: *Pacific and Asia.*

"Lord, what about my team? I can't abandon them." Sensing I should begin reading at Isaiah 40, I continued until I had read through chapter 45. Among many encouraging verses, Isaiah 43:4 spoke to me directly about the question regarding my team: "I will give *other* men in your place and *other* peoples in exchange for your life" (NASB). I knew Africa was over for me. The Pacific and Asia were my new home.

Later I talked to Judi and asked her to consider this change. After prayer she responded, "I feel it's right. We've bonded with the Hawaiian people and our local church. Our kids are doing well. I'm okay with it."

As I relinquished my vision to God, He simultaneously began to expand my vision. He carried the whole world in His heart, and He wanted to enlarge my awareness of it.

NINETEEN

French Polynesia

IN THE spring of 1977, as I recovered my health, I began hearing from people interested in the French Pacific. These included two YWAM staff members in Kona, Corinne and Lee Ann, as well as a young Swiss student named Philippe. I spoke to Loren again about my interest in French Polynesia, New Caledonia, and New Hebrides (now Vanuatu). He encouraged me to pursue what God was opening, so Corinne, Lee Ann, Philippe, and I began praying for our forthcoming ministry. I also put an itinerary together for our team to depart in late June.

I received a letter from Celia, a Hawaiian YWAMer living in Europe. "Joe, God has stirred my heart for the French islands of the Pacific." She wondered why, since no YWAM team was going there. "So I just prayed for the islands. Two weeks ago Cynthia Bloomer said that your team was forming in Hawaii. I received a letter from my friend Lee Ann with all the scriptures you have received in prayer. I believe God wants me with you. I can be in Kona by early June."

My French-speaking team grew to six, including Daniel Schaerer, who would join us in New Caledonia halfway through. Because traveling with two small children into the unknown was tricky, Judi would stay in the States with our children. This ministry trip ended my sabbatical year.

The Lord laid on our team's heart the desire to fellowship with and encourage the local churches in the islands as well as to do evangelism. We wanted to tear down strongholds of darkness through intercession and see possibilities for future teams to minister in the Pacific. We spent time in prayer asking God to show us His priorities. The Lord led us to intercede for discouraged pastors in New Caledonia. We asked the Lord to lead us to them. We also sensed the Lord saying we would be ministering through teaching in New Hebrides.

I found a circle fare out of American Samoa that would allow us to fly to each of the three island nations and back for a very reasonable price. We planned to spend one month in French Polynesia, three weeks in New Caledonia, and two weeks in New Hebrides. We didn't know anyone on the island of Tahiti in French Polynesia, so I sent Corinne and Lee Ann ahead to make contact with the churches, find ministry opportunities, and make housing arrangements.

They wrote saying the main denomination, the Protestant Reformed Church, was not open to working with us. The denomination had been burned by a cult-like group, calling themselves The Children of God. "They played guitars, sang, and stole away our young people," a church leader accused. I remembered the story in Daniel 3 about trusting God even if it meant going through a fiery furnace like Shadrach, Meshach, and Abednego had. "We trust You to open the doors," I declared, "but even if You do not, we will not bow down to the enemy. We trust You, Lord, no matter what."

Once Celia arrived from Switzerland, we departed Kona, arriving in French Polynesia the night of June 21. Unbeknownst to us, the director of the hostel where we were to live had told Corinne we couldn't stay there. With no other options, we booked two rooms in the simple thatched-roofed Te Puna Bel Air Hotel right behind the Faa'a International Airport.

The next morning we gathered for prayer at our hotel in the village of Faa'a. We sensed the Lord telling us to trust Him and to be obedient. I responded, "We will not bow down to the enemy's discouragement. We plant the banner of Jesus in this place. You will be lifted up." Then we asked Him to provide a "man of peace" (Luke 10:6) to open a place for us to stay in town. Our answer came as we contacted a friend of Celia's father who was an official of the tourist board. When he asked, "*Qu'est ce que je peux faire pour vous aider?*" (What can I do to help you?), Celia explained our situation. He made a few phone calls and opened the door for us to stay in the youth hostel for a few days while his assistant worked on finding us a small house to rent for the month. The hostel sat at the mouth of a stream that emptied into the coral-reefed ocean.

The next morning we bought French croissants at a nearby bakery as well as some bananas, papayas, and pineapples at the open air market. Then we met for prayer at the hostel, asking the Lord to lead us again. I saw a picture in my mind of a white trimaran (a sailing boat with a main hull and two outrigger hulls). Explaining the picture to the team, I asked the Lord for direction. Team members prayed for the salvation of the person on that boat. After forty-five minutes we sensed the burden lift and we moved to other prayer subjects.

That afternoon on the way to town, I went by the boat harbor looking for a white trimaran. Sure enough, among all the boats in the harbor there was one trimaran, and it was white. But it was anchored out at a mooring, not tied to the dock, so I couldn't get to it. I watched for twenty minutes to see if someone would come out, but when no one did, I left disappointed.

Each morning we interceded for French Polynesia. Often the Lord gave us specific instructions about what to do and where to minister. This laid the foundation for our ministry.

One morning after our hearts had bonded with the Tahitian people, the Lord invited us to take on a prophetic role like we had done previously in France. Identifying with the sins of the people, we confessed and asked the Lord's forgiveness for them. It was like the prophet did in Daniel 9:3–5, 19: "So I turned to the Lord God and pleaded with him in prayer and petition. . . . I prayed to the LORD my God and confessed: 'O Lord, the great and awesome God, who keeps his covenant of love with all who love him and obey his commands, we have sinned and done wrong. We have been wicked and have rebelled; we have turned away from Your commands and laws. . . . O Lord, listen! O Lord, forgive!'"

Later I found another scripture, Leviticus 26:40–42, that showed God encouraging people to confess the sins of the previous generation: "But if they will confess their sins and the sins of their fathers . . . then when their uncircumcised hearts are humbled and they pay for their sin, I will remember my covenant . . . and I will remember the land."

Many times we prayed for the Christians and tried to connect with the Protestant Reformed Church, but to no avail. Continually we were reminded of the lesson of the fiery furnace. We had to trust God, whether or not He delivered us or opened doors for us. Our job was to keep ministering, despite the enemy's opposition.

I also kept a lookout to see if anyone was on the white trimaran, but no one ever was.

Soon our team moved into a two-bedroom house in a quiet neighborhood, taking a day to clean it, physically and spiritually. The owners lived across the street, giving us opportunities to share our faith both practically and in words. Inviting us over one afternoon, they demonstrated how to husk a coconut by ramming it on a stake with a point like a pickax, drain and save its milk, crack open the inner nut, and rasp its meat into small shreds for cooking and making desserts.

During this time I missed Judi and the kids very much and wrote them often. But Jesus said in Matthew 16:24, "If anyone would come after me, he must deny himself and take up his cross and follow me." The cost of obedience was well worth it.

One Sunday we visited a Tahitian service at the Protestant Reformed Church. Because it was a special service for baptisms, communion, and the dedication of deacons, the women dressed in full-length white gowns with wide-brimmed white hats. Women sat on one side and men on the other. The singing in the service was breathtaking. One woman's soprano voice intoned the melody, and everybody responded in beautiful four-part harmony. Corinne met a British visitor and invited her to our place afterward for a hot drink and further discussion about the Lord. Our house became a focal point for ministry, enabling us to invite many for tea, a meal, and a good conversation about Jesus.

We continued to intercede for the nations daily. The Lord led us to pray for Thailand, former French Indochina (Cambodia, Laos, North and South Vietnam), and refugee camps. We prayed that Christians would see the need of reaching this area of the world for God. "Lord, please call people, including French speakers, to minister to those in the refugee camps in Thailand. Also call people in the refugee camps to be missionaries to their own countries."

The Lord gave Corinne Ezekiel 11:16: "This is what the Sovereign Lord says: Although I sent them far away among the nations and scattered them among the countries, yet for a little while I have been a sanctuary for them in the countries where they have gone." So we prayed that God would be a refuge to the refugees and that YWAM Thailand would understand God's priorities and perspective. "Send to Thailand teachers of Your Word, of spiritual warfare and the character of God. Give the church boldness. Send Your angelic host to battle against the principalities who are thwarting Your purposes there. Show these people You are a God of love." As we prayed, a question stirred me: Would God send *me* to minister to these people someday?

One afternoon Philippe met and witnessed to a Chinese Tahitian named Frank. He came to our house with two of his friends, and we talked to them about the Lord until midnight.

Frank invited us on a tour of the island. We were awed by the beauty of its white-sand beaches, small offshore islands, waterfalls, and majestic and verdant volcanic mountains. We stopped for lunch at his friend's home, and they lavished us with raw fish, vegetables, taro, breadfruit (eaten with coconut milk), grilled steak and chicken, French fries, pineapple, and coffee. After lunch we sat back as Frank and his friend plied us with questions about God and religion. Frank's friend affirmed that he enjoyed hearing us share *les paroles de Dieu* (the words of God).

The following day Frank spent more time with Philippe and me, talking about how to make faith practical. He sat asking questions and hanging on to the answers. We talked again the next afternoon and evening about man's personal responsibility in spiritual things. He visited a couple more times, but sadly he wasn't ready to surrender to Jesus.

During our time in Tahiti we never saw a breakthrough with the church leaders, but we prayed for their people and shared Christ with many hungry hearts. We were encouraged by their openness.

While still in Hawaii, before we had begun our trip, I had written a friend who had visited New Hebrides. Just three days before we left

Tahiti, I received a reply, giving me the name and address of a Christian in Port Vila, the capital city. Though not knowing their situation, I immediately sent this person, Philip, a letter saying we felt God's direction to be in New Hebrides from August 6 to 22. Because of the shortness of time to reply, I asked him to respond to me in New Caledonia. Then I focused my attention on wrapping things up in Tahiti and preparing for our flight to the next country of ministry.

Our new friends brought us to the airport and gave us shell leis. When we finally boarded our plane and sat down, I again committed the person on the white trimaran to the Lord. *I don't know what You've done in answer to our prayers, but I trust You and release that person into Your hands.* I looked out the window. *Now I'll never find out what happened on that boat.*

As the plane gained altitude, I leaned back in my seat and my mind switched forward. We didn't know anyone in New Caledonia, and I wondered what awaited us there.

TWENTY

New Caledonia and Vanuatu

ARRIVING in New Caledonia on July 19, we caught a bus into Nouméa, the capital. "What will we be doing here?" asked one student as we booked two rooms in an inexpensive hotel, one for the guys and one for the girls.

"I don't know exactly," I replied. "I don't have any contacts here, but I'm trusting God to guide us."

The next day we interceded for the country. We asked God to open the doors and show us what He wanted us to do. Then we set out to explore this new place.

The following day we prayed but received no direction. I panicked. "Lord, I have a team that will get discouraged quickly if we flounder with no direction. Please show me the next step." Waiting quietly, the thought came to me, *Go down to the street and turn right.* I pleaded with the Lord for more understanding, but that was all I got. So I took one of the team members, Philippe, and walked down the stairs from our second-floor rooms and at the sidewalk turned right. The city was built on a hill, so we slowly climbed, traversing many cross streets till we reached the top. A Protestant Reformed Church sat at the apex of the hill. Entering the gate, we met a gardener trimming flowers in the well-manicured grounds. "May I help you?" he asked.

"We want to connect with the pastors, find out your spiritual needs and how we can help."

"Just wait about five minutes and the person you want to see will arrive," he replied.

We looked at each other a little confused. Five minutes later a car drove up, and the gardener presented us to a pastor. He introduced himself as the General Secretary of the Protestant Reformed Church. He couldn't stay long but invited us to his home the following night for dinner.

As Philippe and I walked down the hill back into town, we noticed a sign in a second-floor window that said *Librairie Chrétienne* (Christian Bookstore). Climbing the stairs, we entered a large room filled with bookshelves and spoke with a couple, Peter and Jean, from New Zealand who ran it. With welcoming smiles they invited our team to a Bible study that evening in their home. God seemed to be directing us differently here than in Tahiti. We sensed Him saying, "Trust Me. 'I will counsel you with My eye upon you' (Psalm 32:8 NASB)."

Around 7:00 PM Peter picked us up. At his home we met several missionary couples and local Melanesian pastors, many from the Protestant Free Church. Peter invited us to speak. I explained our purpose in coming and introduced the ministry of YWAM. People from the house fellowship spoke next. A young teacher named José and his wife, Kathy, worked part-time with the Bible Society. They said they gave out Christian literature at church book tables, especially bush churches in the interior of the island. A French couple, Guy and Astride, taught in a Catholic school and told us about the patience they learned while trying to start a Bible club there. Peter told how God had led him and his wife to begin the bookstore to serve New Caledonian churches. He also mentioned he had met a YWAM team from New Zealand some ten years before.

Then others talked about New Caledonia, explaining the tribal structure of the Melanesian society with chiefs in each village, a head chief over each district, and their council of elders. The communal culture had little room for individualism. Nouméa was the big city, but tribal villages, many without electricity or running water, populated the interior.

During a tea and fellowship time afterward, José asked where we were staying. When I mentioned the hotel, he immediately said, "No, that's not right. Come stay in our home. The Lord has blessed us with a spacious house, with enough room for everyone." When I hesitated, he said, "We won't accept no for an answer. We'll pick you up tomorrow morning at your hotel."

"Thank you very much. That's such a blessing." And it was. We didn't have enough money to cover the hotel for many more days. The next morning we moved.

Responding to the invitation we received the previous day, Philippe and I went to dinner that evening at the house of the General Secretary of the Protestant Reformed Church. As he unveiled his tender heart for his people, we were knit together as Christian brothers. He told us he had been sent to France for training at the Faculty of Theology, but by a clerical error he ended up at an evangelical Bible school outside Paris. While there, he surrendered his life to Jesus. As General Secretary of the denomination now, he tried to introduce his fellow pastors to what he had experienced of the Lord. Most were not interested. Expressing his discouragement, he confided he was considering resigning.

A strong word of encouragement for him rose in my spirit. "God cares for you. He has seen your pain and sent us across the Pacific to say for Him, 'Don't give up. You are representing My heart in this difficult place. Keep persevering.'" I concluded with, "God is here with you. He will strengthen and help you. Please don't give up; your people and your country need you." As we left, I thought, *This must have been one of the pastors God led us to pray for back in Kona. If we came across the Pacific just for this one person, this trip was well worth it.*

As our team sat around a long dining room table and talked with José and Kathy, our new hosts, we learned more about the churches in New Caledonia. The Protestant Reformed Church was more liberal in its theology, and twenty years before, a group split from it to form the Protestant Free Church. Now that church was experiencing its own problems. Some of the young pastors and missionaries were struggling with what they felt was a drift from their original values. Things were tense, and many were asking what they should do.

On Monday we met with a Protestant Free Church pastor, who expressed the church's need for solid biblical teaching. Then he talked about tensions within the church. We encouraged and prayed for him. *Another discouraged pastor. Thank You, Lord, for leading us to him.*

That evening Guy and Astride invited our team and several missionaries and pastors from the Protestant Free Church to dinner. They, too, were struggling with denominational tensions. Church leaders were polarized. Some had been removed from their posts and were walking through the pain of dying dreams. I felt like weeping with them. I sensed the Lord wanting to bring healing, if both sides laid down their arms.

"God led us to pray for you before we came to New Caledonia. He has not forgotten or rejected you," I said. Aware this church was verging on a split, I encouraged them to choose unity. From the story of David and King Saul, I shared how David refused to "touch God's anointed," even when Saul tried to kill him. In God's timing, David found his place of leadership without causing a rebellion, showing a godly way to bring change in an ungodly situation. I encouraged them not to compromise truth, but to walk righteously in their suffering. Then we prayed together. Again I thought, *Thank You, Lord, for leading us once again to discouraged pastors.*

As our team sang and testified to children and young people in the schools and churches, pastors and missionaries in the Protestant Free Church opened doors for us to minister in the interior of the island in various tribal villages.

We still hadn't heard from Daniel Schaerer, who was supposed to join us here in New Caledonia. The Central Post Office had a place to receive letters for people without a local post box, at a window called *Poste Restante* (mail left till claimed), where I sent and received letters to and from Judi. We checked there daily for a letter with Daniel's arrival information, but walked away empty-handed each time. Since the airport was nearly forty miles away and we didn't have a vehicle, I phoned and paged at the arrival of every overseas flight. But no one ever answered.

At noon on Wednesday, Guy and Astride invited us to their home for lunch. During our conversation we mentioned we hadn't heard from an arriving team member and didn't know when he would come. We asked if they would keep an eye out for him, because we were leaving the next day for the interior. "We left a letter for him this morning at the *Poste Restante* window," I explained. "Hopefully he'll check it when he finds we're gone."

"Let me drive you to the airport. You can leave a note for him there," Guy responded.

"Thank you, Guy, but that's way too far."

"Absolutely not. Let us do that for you," Astride interjected.

"Anyway," Guy blurted out, "Qantas is flying its inaugural 747 flight to Nouméa this afternoon. If we hurry, we can leave a message and watch that huge plane land. I want to see that."

An hour later Guy, Philippe, and I arrived at the airport and posted our note. "Come on, Joe," Guy exclaimed, "let's head up to the observation deck. If we're quick, we can see the Qantas plane arrive."

As we reached the observation area, we saw the descent of a huge plane bearing the Qantas insignia. A small puff of white smoke sprung up behind the wheels as they touched the runway. The plane slowed, taxiing to its parking spot in front of us. The ground crew brought stairs to the plane's door, and soon passengers began climbing down to the tarmac and walking toward the entry door just below us. We started to turn away to head back home when I noticed a familiar face. "Hey, guys, wait a minute," I called.

When the arriving passenger reached the tarmac, he looked up and waved at me. Standing before me was Daniel Schaerer. He smiled warmly like he was expecting us. At that distance he couldn't see the startled look in my eyes. *How on earth did he get on a Qantas flight coming from Australia?* I wondered. *He's supposed to be coming from France.*

"I'm glad you came," Daniel began as he walked up to us. "I didn't know how to find you. You got my letter?"

"No, we never received your letter. We didn't know you were arriving today." I explained how we just "happened" to be at the airport, and we all rejoiced in God's care.

The next day we took an old beat-up bus over a dirt road to an interior village. Of the nearly 1,680 miles of roads in New Caledonia at that time, only about 155 miles were paved. That left 1,525 miles of rutted dirt roads. That week we criss-crossed the island, ministering in various villages, until we arrived in the town of Houailou (pronounced "why-lou"), where we found the headquarters of the Protestant Free Church.

In a village just outside of Houailou with no electricity or running water, the president of the Protestant Free Church received our team into his home so we could minister in his church over the weekend. At first I was very nervous, since I had heard the struggles many of the pastors and missionaries were going through within that church. I worried that God was going to have us rebuke this church leader for the suffering of his people.

To my joy this gracious man received us as honored guests, having all our meals prepared over an open fire in the cooking shed behind his house. We talked for hours, sitting at his table illuminated by kerosene lanterns. As he shared his concerns and his desire that his people once again experience the revelation of the Holy Spirit through the Word of God, I encouraged him to keep pursuing this desire. He wanted his young people to live their faith practically, not just perform outward signs of "churchianity." I responded, "God sees your heart. Don't give up. Keep seeking your people's welfare." *Another pastor to encourage.*

During this time I almost fell into the trap of taking sides—deciding one group was more right than the other. But I learned that God doesn't choose sides in such conflicts; He is above them. He sees suffering people on both sides and appeals to both to walk in His ways and seek reconciliation and unity.

On Wednesday, August 3, we made the five-hour bus trip back to Nouméa. Finding a telegram from Port Vila, New Hebrides, I read they were having a Charismatic Conference from August 8 to 13 and wanted us to be involved. We would arrive two days before the conference and be there a week afterward. God's timing was perfect. I sent off a quick letter to Judi about our time.

During our last two days in New Caledonia we reconnected with many of our new friends and spoke in a couple more church services. Our last evening the Bible study group from the bookstore came to our house for a farewell. We shared, sang, and worshiped the Lord together one final time. The next day a procession of four cars took us to the airport. As we drove, I silently poured out my thanks to the Lord. *I'm amazed at what You did in three short weeks. You opened many doors, introduced us to scores of wonderful people, and enabled us to express Your heart to the church of this country.*

EXITING the plane in Port Vila, we were greeted by a gust of warm air. When we cleared immigration, Philip, our contact, met and took us to the home he rented at a beautiful estate overlooking the bay. One of the three conference speakers had gotten sick and flown home that morning. Philip asked, "Would you be one of the speakers? We believe God sent you here just for that."

"Of course," I responded. Then panicking I thought, *Lord, what can I speak on?*

New Hebrides was made up of over eighty islands. Its British-French government included three official languages: English, French, and Bislama (a form of Pidgin English and French). With 113 indigenous languages, Bislama became the one spoken by the majority of the Melanesians. To tell people I didn't speak it, I would say, "Me no savy toktok Bislama."

Many New Hebrides factions were pushing for immediate independence, and one group had already declared itself free from the colonial governments. Some of the Christians expressed their concern that if these factions tried to force independence, there would be much bloodshed.

That afternoon we joined a group from the charismatic renewal in the city gathered at Philip's house, worshiping in Bislama. A traditional feast followed. Local dishes of fish, pork, chicken, taro, breadfruit, yams, and manioc sat on a banana leaf "tablecloth" covering the floor. Papayas, bananas, mangoes, and pineapples followed.

After the meal they began singing again, followed by prayer for those wanting healing or just a blessing from the Lord. I began praying for the first person with a very eloquent prayer that went nowhere. *Pray to Me for this person, or go and sit down,* God said to my mind.

I began in earnest, focusing on God and calling out to Him. I pictured His hand reaching out from heaven. As I prayed, the hand came down until I sensed it touch the head of the person for whom I was praying. I waited to hear a "Hallelujah." Instead, the person collapsed on the floor, seemingly lost in the presence of the Lord. I had never seen this before, and I was so startled I stopped praying and sat down in a nearby chair. I felt the Lord challenge me to step out on a limb and allow Him to "expand my borders" in ministry. So I got back up and continued praying for people.

The conference began two days later with four scheduled meetings each day. I spoke at one, and the team led a worship and music workshop for another. I still struggled when people collapsed while I prayed for them, but I persisted after hearing them testify about what God did in their hearts when they were "lost" in His presence. I asked God to expand my borders and teach me more about spiritual ministry. Wanting to cultivate a teachable spirit, I guarded my heart so that I didn't pull back from things I didn't understand.

One morning in the teepee-shaped auditorium of the Paton Memorial Presbyterian Church, I challenged the people to become intercessors, standing in the gap on behalf of their nation (according to Ezekiel 22:30) to keep judgment from it. The speaker in the next session challenged them similarly. Then he called for a public stand, and more than twenty people came forward to commit themselves to intercede for their nation. In Ezekiel 22, God was looking for one man. We rejoiced that in New Hebrides twenty responded. Three years later on July 30, 1980, amid minor conflicts but no major bloodbaths, the two colonial powers granted New Hebrides independence, making it the Republic of Vanuatu.

During that conference we met briefly with the general assembly of the Presbyterian pastors of New Hebrides. With over 60 percent of the nation being members of the Presbyterian Church, the pastors exerted a very strong political influence. Later we met with the president of the National Political Party, the strongest party at that time. At the end of the conference we were amazed; we had arrived in the country eight days before, not knowing anyone, yet God had opened so many doors of ministry.

The week following the conference our team taught some of the young leaders of the charismatic renewal. We were not here to take over but to come alongside these people and help them fulfill their calling and vision. Multiplication meant raising up new leaders, not doing more ourselves.

We rejoiced together as a team about all God had done throughout the summer. Then, passing briefly through Fiji and Samoa, we arrived back in Kona on August 22.

Back at home I reconnected and played with Lisa and Joey before I sat down with Judi and told her about the three countries we had ministered in. It was so important to ask God how to minister in each one. Though all were in the South Pacific, each was totally different, having its own spiritual needs, based on its own history and its people's choices. Because of this, God gave us different types of ministry in each place. He also spoke to us differently in each place.

Judi puzzled over this. "What do you mean, Joe?"

"In Tahiti God directed us daily in prayer, while in New Caledonia He opened doors as we stepped out." I also told Judi of the resistance we experienced in Tahiti. But in the midst of the challenges, we enjoyed the presence of Jesus with us, just like Daniel's three friends did in the fiery furnace. God, I was learning, desires our trust and obedience in specific circumstances, and He won't let us put Him in a box about the way He guides us.

TWENTY-ONE

A Grain of Wheat

LESS than a month after my return to Kona, on September 15, 1977, YWAM purchased the bankrupt and abandoned Pacific Empress Hotel. For us it was the crossing of the Jordan River into our Promised Land. We had prayed and worked hard for the past couple of years for a place to establish our ministries, and now that day had come. I began serving on the YWAM Kona leadership team as well as targeting the French Pacific.

That fall I accepted an invitation to teach at YWAM's French School of Evangelism in Switzerland. I decided I would first stop in Montreal to teach at the YWAM school there, then go on to Europe, and then to Africa, where I would tell my friends about the changes that had occurred in my life. I also needed to liquidate the two households of belongings we had left behind—one packed in barrels in Lausanne that had been destined for shipment to Africa, and the other in M'Pouto. The YWAM leadership in Europe had made the decision to keep the M'Pouto center open after all, because the team had chosen to continue the work there, and others had joined them in that vision. During my trip, Judi would remain in Kona with Lisa, who was almost five, and Joey, who was two and a half.

I wondered how I could explain adequately why I wouldn't be returning to work in Africa. I asked the Lord many times over the following weeks to give me understanding about this change of direction. John 12:24 was the only response I received: "Unless a grain of wheat falls into the earth and dies, it remains alone; but if it dies, it bears much fruit" (NASB). That, however, didn't make sense to me. *Lord, that doesn't answer my question. What does that mean?* No understanding came.

On November 7, I arrived at the Dunham YWAM center just outside of Montreal, which had been established through YWAM's Olympic Games outreach the previous year. Autumn colors decorated the trees, and a thick blanket of fallen leaves covered the ground beneath them. Coming from the tropical climate of Hawaii, I had forgotten how invigorating the crisp air could feel and how beautiful fall could be.

Before teaching at the school, I spent time with René LaFramboise, the straightforward but kind director of the French work in Quebec. He had attended the School of Evangelism in Lausanne, Switzerland, two years before, and had led one of our teams to Brittany, France. I sat on a beige sofa in René's apartment as his wife Christiane poured me a cup of tea. We talked about what he had done over the last couple of years. Then René stretched out in his burnt-orange armchair, peered over his wire-rimmed glasses, and asked the question I had been dreading. "Well, Joe, what about Africa? What happened?"

I looked down at my cup of tea and traced a ring around its lip with my finger. "I've spent a year trying to figure that one out myself. But I haven't explained my thoughts to anyone besides Judi."

"If you'd rather not talk about it, that's perfectly all right," René broke in.

"No, no, René. That's okay. I need to try. I'm going to have to anyway when I get to Europe and Africa. I don't have it all worked out yet, but let me share what little I do know. This past year I've been walking through a dark valley, like what David referred to in Psalm 23:4 as the 'valley of the shadow of death.' I had no idea why I got sick and couldn't return to Africa. I had been doing the right thing in Africa, obeying God's direction in my life."

"But, Joe," René interrupted, "how could you end up in such a mess by doing the right thing? It doesn't make sense to me."

"Don't feel bad; it doesn't make a lot of sense to me either."

Fumbling for answers as we talked, I explained what happened in Wisconsin and how I had arrived in Hawaii mad at God. I told about that afternoon when I made my peace with God, quit fighting, and stopped trying to escape the valley. "But," I admitted, "for that valley to be any help to me, God saw that I needed to hold His hand and let Him lead and teach me through it."

I was startled by the next thought that came. In God's love, at the entrance to the valley a year ago, I realized that He must have been saying to me, *Joe, look at what you have in your hand.* It was, of course, my burden and vision for Africa. *You have to let go of it so you will have an empty hand to take hold of Mine. That way I can lead you through the valley.* My throat constricted, and tears brimmed in my eyes. I had not realized before that very moment that this was what had been happening. All I knew was that I had to let go of my vision for Africa and trust in God's faithfulness and love. I now saw that God had been good and loving, and He had been trying to help me the whole time.

René peered into my eyes with compassion, letting me unfold my painful thoughts. I coughed and cleared my throat two or three times to avoid sounding like how I felt. I explained to René that when I quit fighting and took His hand in the "valley," God began to teach me about Himself and the depth of trust He wanted me to have in Him. It was for my good. Valley times have to come because God wants to give us something better.

Then I remembered something Loren once told me. He said that God entrusts us with more spiritual responsibility as we grow in spiritual maturity. I told René that a scripture the Lord gave me this year summed this up: "Unless a grain of wheat falls into the earth and dies, it remains alone; but if it dies, it bears much fruit" (John 12:24 NASB). This death process, I now realized as René and I talked, developed maturity.

Looking at my watch, I saw it was time to leave. "René, I appreciate this time we've had. Your questions have helped me put some of this together before I go to Europe and Africa. Thanks."

René asked to pray and declared over me, "Be in the French world as a man of peace and a reconciler, bringing unity where there was division." As I left René's apartment, I couldn't get John 12:24 out of my mind. It seemed that "death" was the price for "much fruit."

When I arrived in Switzerland, the forest on the outskirts of Lausanne next to the YWAM center was also draped in gorgeous autumn colors. Arriving a week before I was to teach, I brushed up on my language skills so I could teach in French, and I continued preparing the fifteen hours of lectures I would give.

I had on my heart to teach principles people could use for pioneering new mission fields. The following afternoon as I reflected on Judi and my personal experiences, I remembered the promises we had received from the Lord through Ezekiel 36 and 37 for revival in France. When Ezekiel prophesied in the valley of dry bones, not only did the bones form bodies that eventually came to life, but the living bodies were raised up as a mighty army. I had not yet seen revival or that mighty army. The first team of six people I led to France saw one convert. The second team, nineteen people, saw two or three converts. The third team, twenty people, saw fifteen to twenty converts but no revival. The following years we saw more teams involved but still no revival.

How can I teach this subject when I've not seen the fulfillment of the promises I received seven years ago for revival in France? I wondered. *Have I been doing something wrong?* I knelt down beside the bed in my room. "Lord, I feel so inadequate to teach in this school. Please help me understand why we haven't seen revival in France yet."

As I quieted my soul in the Lord's presence, a memory popped into my mind. It had taken place during the summer when I was sixteen years old. I got a job as a laborer for a construction company that was building a two-story apartment complex. The stairs, coming down from the top floor to the ground floor, were anchored into a four-foot by four-foot cement slab that had been poured too high. When people came down the stairs, they would stumble on the last step because the distance to the cement landing was different from all the other steps.

My boss called me over, handed me a large sledge hammer, and told me to break out the cement landing so it could be poured again at the proper height. I studied the slab for a moment. I told myself, *I'll bet I can break this slab with one blow of this sledge hammer.* So I raised the hammer over my head, focused all my attention on the slab, let out a shout, and swung the hammer down with all my force.

To my utter shock, it didn't budge.

Maybe it'll take two blows. So I raised the hammer over my head a second time and with all my strength swung it down. To my amazement, absolutely nothing happened. I stepped back a moment and decided I had to just keep swinging the hammer until it broke. I struck the slab five times, ten times, fifteen times, twenty times. I lost count. I don't know how many blows it took. Let's just say somewhere around the forty-third blow, cracks appeared. Then it took only two or three more blows on the larger hunks until I could lift out all the pieces.

Reflecting on that event, I sensed the Lord ask, "Which blow of the hammer broke the slab?" Then understanding came to my mind: it was all the blows.

God was saying to me, "France is spiritually like a cement slab, hard and immovable. But every time you go into France with a team, you are swinging the hammer and striking a blow. That is all I ask of you. Keep persevering and striking the hardened slab. Every time pastors and evangelists preach in France, they are striking a blow. One day the slab will break—revival will come. Every blow will have contributed to that. Man may try to analyze what technique the last person used when revival came, but I don't look at it that way. For every person who struck the slab, I will say, 'Well done, good and faithful servant; you were faithful over a few things, I will make you ruler over many things. Enter into the joy of your lord' (Matt. 25:21 NKJV)."

My job was to faithfully strike the slab each time I was given the opportunity. Only God knew when it would break. One day revival would come to France.

More understanding came later when I read Jeremiah 23:29, "'Is not my word like fire,' declares the LORD, 'and like a hammer that breaks a rock in pieces?'" I realized that the countries we go into may be hard like a rock, but God's word is like a hammer. I also found Hebrews 11:13, "All these people were still living by faith when they died. They did not receive the things promised; they only saw them and welcomed them from a distance." I began to see that, with France, revival might take several generations, but it would come—if not in my generation, in a following one.

That next week God gave me a new authority to teach how making a difference in a country requires perseverance above almost anything else. Along with teaching on principles for pioneering into new places, I challenged the students to expand their vision to consider the entire French-speaking world as their mission field. With excitement I could see the bigger picture, the potential of multiplication through these people.

Also during the teaching week I shared my story about Africa and what I had learned over the past year. Many people asked me what happened. Now I could explain using the same scriptures that had come so full of meaning that afternoon in René's apartment in Canada.

I was also able to talk in more detail with several special friends. Daniel Schaerer, having resigned his teaching position, was working full time with YWAM in Lausanne. André Sivager was there getting ready for his wedding. Though no longer with YWAM, he and his wife-to-be, Hélène, had many friends in Lausanne, making it the ideal place for their upcoming marriage. Tom Bloomer preached in the ceremony, and I had the privilege of leading them in their vows and pronouncing them husband and wife.

The following week I worked daily on sorting through all we had left in our apartment and the twelve barrels we had packed for shipment to Africa. Judi wanted me to give our few pieces of furniture to various friends. Daniel Schaerer was preparing to take a team to France to open our first YWAM center there, so I gave them most of our household belongings. Then I repacked the few things I would bring back to Hawaii, amazed at all we had accumulated. Judi and I had arrived in Europe for the first time eight years before, each with only one green forty-four-pound suitcase.

At the end of the week, I left for West Africa, carrying a roll of window screening in my baggage to mosquito-proof the house in M'Pouto, even though I wouldn't be staying. In spite of the more complete understanding about my redirection from Africa that I had acquired in Canada from talking to René, I still couldn't quiet the disappointment I felt. My stomach knotted as I thought of returning to the place I had worked so hard to prepare for my family and team, the place I thought would be the fulfillment of over twenty years of anticipation. Most of all, I wondered what was happening with those I'd left behind.

As soon as I stepped off the plane that evening in Abidjan, the oppressive weight of hot, humid air hit me, so different from the cool autumn I had just left in Switzerland. My clothes stuck to my clammy skin. I had forgotten how unpleasant that could feel. I was back in West Africa.

The YWAM team greeted me when I cleared immigration and customs. Along with the familiar faces of the team, I saw two African faces. One totally unfamiliar to me belonged to a young man introduced to me as Lamine Dembélé. The second I immediately recognized as the young albino I had seen in our village last year. His name was Isaac Berté. Both from the village of M'Pouto, they had become Christians through the work of our team during the past year. Isaac, led to the Lord by André Sivager, was friendly and jovial, always smiling. Lamine appeared more serious-natured. They were the two students in our first Discipleship Training School in French West Africa. Though small, this school was the beginning of the fulfillment of my dream of training Africans for missions.

Driving out the northeast end of Abidjan toward M'Pouto, I found myself in familiar surroundings. But when we arrived at the front of our house, I could not believe my eyes. What had been an empty sandy lot with a few mango trees surrounding our house was now a green paradise of trees, shrubs, flowers, and lawn. The front gate, cut into a hedge, opened to a flagstone path that curved a quarter-circle turn through the lawn to the front porch, like a storybook picture.

Once inside the house, I walked over and turned on the faucet to try out the homemade water system. It had been completed five months after my family and I departed. Though the water pressure was not strong, it worked well. Each day someone pumped water up the tower to fill the barrel. Most days filling the tank once was sufficient.

I sat in my mosquito-netted bed that first night and wrote a letter to Judi by the dim light of my flashlight. The paper stuck to my sweaty hands, smudging the ink. But it felt good to talk to Judi, even if only by letter. I woke up once in the night hearing the buzz of mosquitoes hurling themselves against the net trying to get in. Then to my chagrin I discovered three or four on the inside. I must not have tucked the net in well. Wondering if they could be carrying malaria, I spent quite a while chasing and killing those mosquitoes before I could go back to sleep.

The next morning I talked to the team, along with Isaac and Lamine, beginning with my testimony of what I had learned over the past year. Even though I wept throughout the time, it was easier to share with them, since I had already shared the same story in Canada and in Europe. I also spent time praying for them. Their openness and receptivity were so refreshing.

I met with M. Bernard, the owner of our house. By this time he had married a sixth wife, who came regularly to see our nurses regarding her health. I also met with some other neighbors. Then I emptied the box shipped from the States. Cockroaches had eaten the birthday candles sent for our children, but everything else had survived. A few items I packed into my suitcase, but most I left, making the change all the more final. I would not live and work with this team again.

On my last night we had a celebration banquet to praise God for all He had done thus far and to declare our belief in all He was yet to do. We finished by praying over Isaac and Lamine that God would fulfill every desire of their hearts and use them to start new ministries in West Africa.

Late that night, with a feeling of peace and satisfaction I boarded the plane for my return trip to Europe and America. Sitting in my seat waiting for the plane to take off, I waved enthusiastically out the window at the staff and the two students on the observation deck. God was doing something here. He was doing it through these people.

TWENTY-TWO

Challenges and Joys

IN THE summer of 1978 I had the opportunity to go to one area of the French-speaking world I had not touched—South America and the Caribbean. I first flew to Argentina for a YWAM outreach at the World Cup Games. We distributed 150,000 pieces of literature, held open-air meetings, and saw many people come to the Lord. After a challenging and exciting month, I departed Buenos Aires to do some mission trailblazing.

My first French destination was Cayenne, French Guyana. When I reached the airport I only had ten dollars left. My contacts there were not at the airport, so I decided to take a taxi to their house. The driver said the fare would be ten dollars. I sat in the back seat with waves of panic sweeping over me. *What if I can't find their house? What will I do? How will I get back to the airport tomorrow with no money?*

The driver found their home, but the lights were out. I got out of the taxi and walked up to the house, which looked like a small fortified hacienda. A solid-wood front door with no windows hung on huge strap hinges. No one answered my frantic pounding. *This must be a security door covering another door behind it.*

After the taxi driver pounded on the door, also without success, he took me to a hotel that I hoped would take a credit card. Unfortunately, none of the few hotels in town would. Since it was so late by now, I asked the driver if I could just sleep in his car. With a kind heart he brought me to a hotel he knew, negotiated with the manager for a ten-dollar room, and handed the hotel manager the money I had paid him for the taxi ride. Though the room was sparse, with hardly more than a saggy single bed and a bathroom out in the hallway, I was very grateful. Praying a blessing on the taxi cab driver that night, I asked the Lord to help me complete the trip.

The next morning I did connect with my contact and learned about the needs of that nation. Later that day I flew on to Fort-de-France, Martinique, where I was met by a couple in whose Discipleship Training School (YWAM's introductory training program) I had taught the previous year in Switzerland. I spent a couple of days with them, hearing about their ministry and encouraging them in the spiritual challenges of their island. On the ride back to the airport, I began to worry about how I would finish this trip with no money. I had not told my hosts that I was out of cash, so I was surprised and delighted when they handed me a twenty-dollar bill. Realizing the sacrifice this involved, I thanked them profusely. They probably had no idea how significant that provision was for me.

From Martinique, I flew via Guadeloupe and St. Martin (a Dutch/French island) to Port-au-Prince, Haiti, where I encountered overwhelming poverty. At its root was a spiritual poverty unlike anything I had experienced. I learned that in launching their slave rebellion against the French colonial government in 1791, the leaders sealed their compact with a voodoo ceremony a week before the uprising began. Though 80 percent of the population claimed to be Catholic and 15 to 20 percent Protestant, over half the population practiced voodoo. This spiritual darkness still hung over the country like a dark storm cloud and troubled my spirit deeply. I was glad to leave, returning to my family in Kona. (Thankfully, today YWAM has a strong ministry presence there.)

BACK in Kona, life seemed to be smiling on our family and ministry. Near the end of 1978 Judi gave birth to our third child, an energetic boy with brown eyes and a full head of dark hair, Daniel Loren, born in Kealakekua, Hawaii. A couple of months later I flew to Switzerland, where I had been invited to teach in the Lausanne School of Evangelism. To my great delight, I learned that Daniel Schaerer had just become engaged to my former administrative assistant, Maguy. Also to my delight, it seemed that every day I met more people whom God was calling to the French-speaking world. One was DTS student Jean-Patrick Perrin, a tall young man with a heart to serve the Lord. I prayed for God to help him step out in ministry. "I'm looking forward to meeting you on the mission field someday," I said. I also had the chance to talk with Dave and Doris Snider, a couple perfecting their French to go to French Polynesia, and told them about my team's time in Tahiti.

Following that week in Switzerland, I flew to Ivory Coast for one last visit with my former team. I spent a lot of time with Isaac and Lamine again, counseling and praying for them. Lamine told me he had gone through the initiation rites in his village as a boy. Now he was haunted in his dreams by the village elders telling him he still belonged to them. I took authority with him over those tormenting powers of darkness and commanded them to leave, declaring, "He is a child of God now, and no longer belongs to you." That night he slept a little better. Before I left M'Pouto, I encouraged Lamine to keep resisting the enemy until the battle fully lifted.

Traveling back through Europe, I attended an "If My People" concert based on 2 Chronicles 7:14, put on by our French music team. They called the church back to prayer, humility, and unity so God's blessing would flow on the land. I thought of those prayer meetings we had in the early days. God often led us to pray for unity in the churches of France. *We can discover God's heart and some of our strategies for ministry out of the content of our intercession times,* I thought. *We have to listen closely as God directs our prayers.*

Stopping through Paris on my return to the United States, I visited Daniel and Maguy Schaerer and YWAM France's first center in a little farming village one and a half hours outside of Paris. A former orphanage, the land and buildings were given to YWAM outright. Walking through the village, I studied the four large manor houses, a bungalow, and the chapel building that made up this gift. There was land to plant gardens and plenty of rooms to house our people. This was so much more than the farmhouse I had wanted to buy in 1973 to house our summer outreach. God had focused me on developing the ministry before trying to get a center through Proverbs 24:27, "Finish your outdoor work and get your fields ready; after that, build your house." It was well worth the wait. In the coming years this center would train over three thousand young people and send them to more than sixty countries.

Back in Kona in February 1979, I received a letter from the team leader in M'Pouto. I opened it eagerly, but the news inside left me stunned. It read, "I have very sad news. Our dear friend Lamine Dembélé came down with hepatitis a few weeks ago. Before he had fully recovered, he visited his family village up north. While there, he had a relapse. We drove up and brought him to a mission hospital nearby. However, he had been so weakened that the doctors couldn't save him. In less than three weeks he died."

I sat down hard, and the letter fell from my hand. *That's impossible. I was just with him. He was so alive and full of potential, with such a strong desire to grow in God and become a minister.* As I wept, the Lord reminded me of John 12:24, where the grain of wheat falls to the ground and dies. Jesus said that if it did, it would bring forth much fruit. Lamine must have been one of those precious seeds. I didn't know there was still more suffering to come.

IN THE spring I began working with the Small Boat Ministry in Kona, with the goal of bringing the gospel to small islands in the Pacific where air transport was impossible. One day I received a phone call from a DTS student named Larry wanting to find out how to get involved in this ministry. The next afternoon, perched on our floral-patterned sofa, he introduced himself as a marine biologist and sailor. After listening for a while, I asked Larry how he met the Lord.

"Well, it's unusual," he began. "Almost two years ago I was sailing in the South Pacific and anchored in Fiji next to the *Dayspring*, a boat belonging to the South Pacific Bible Society. The skipper handed me a

Bible, which I put away and promptly forgot about. I wasn't interested in spiritual or religious things. Then I cruised to Tahiti and anchored in Papeete harbor."

"Two years ago, during the summer of 1977?" I asked with awakening realization.

"Why, yes, it was," he continued. "While sitting out in the harbor, for some strange reason I brought out that Bible and began reading it. The more I read, the more I wanted to read. I can't explain why this sudden interest, but for hours I was drawn to it. The more I read, the more alive it became. I decided to yield my life to God. So I prayed and met Jesus. Peace filled my heart."

I sat up on the edge of my chair. "What kind of boat were you sailing?"

"A trimaran."

My voice now choked with emotion. "What color was it?"

Looking a little startled at my reaction, he answered slowly, "It was white. Why?"

Through my tears, I told him how God led us to pray for the salvation of a person on a white trimaran in Papeete harbor the summer of 1977. I assured him I would love to have him work with us in the Small Boat Ministry. And he did.

During this time I tried to find out as much as I could about the South Pacific Islands. My friends Dave and Doris had completed their language study in France and were serving as missionaries in French Polynesia. In their ministry newsletter Dave mentioned he had prayed for a sick Tahitian elder and God had healed him. This man gave his life to the Lord, and through his testimony, over twenty from his village also did. This eventually developed into a church in the village of Faa'a. When I read this, I couldn't contain my joy. I excitedly called Judi.

"Listen, Sweetheart. Dave and Doris are building a church in Faa'a."

Judi was a little puzzled. "Explain to me why that's so exciting to you, please."

"In 1977 when we arrived in Tahiti, we spent our first night at a hotel in that village. The next morning we began a prayer battle for Tahiti, taking authority over the enemy in Jesus' name. In faith we spiritually planted the flag of God's kingdom there. That first prayer meeting had more effect than I realized. This church is a little part of our inheritance too."

After walking through the pain of Lamine's death a few months before, it was reassuring to see tangible manifestations that God was still on the throne. Seeing such specific answers to prayer gave me the conviction that God heard and answered—in His way—every prayer He led us to pray, whether or not we ever saw it. I was reminded of what I had learned in France, that prayer is God's invitation for us to enter into His plans. Prayer is not trying to convince a reluctant God to do something He doesn't want to do. Nor is it informing an uninformed God about something He doesn't know. He knows and wants to act, and He is trying to get our attention to pray what is in His heart. As we pray, we enter into the flow of history with Him.

While participating in the South Pacific Games outreach in Suva, Fiji, from August 20 to September 12, 1979, I met the skipper of the Bible Society's *Dayspring*. He was the man who handed Larry a Bible in Fiji two years before. I told him the rest of Larry's story.

"Did you try to talk to Larry about the Lord?" I asked.

"No, I just handed him a Bible," the skipper confessed.

"God used that Bible to change Larry's life," I said, affirming that act.

Returning to the school where we were housed during the outreach, I heard Loren speak about a visit that he, Joy Dawson, and Don Stephens had just made to a refugee camp in Thailand. He challenged us to respond to the needs of those people, both physical and spiritual. I remembered the prayer meeting we had in Tahiti two years before, and how God had touched my heart for those refugees. Was God now wanting me to get involved in this situation?

TWENTY-THREE

A Burden for Refugees

UPON my return to Kona, my attention turned to the Small Boat Ministry and our School of Navigation. At the start of our school, the Lord laid on the heart of a student to pray for the Southeast Asian "boat people" and the Cambodian refugees during our intercession time. We joined together, praying, "Lord, release Your message of the gospel hand-in-hand with physical help. Release Christian doctors and nurses. Move by Your Holy Spirit among the Khmer Rouge." This subject came up in prayer several times over the next week.

On October 10, as I sought the Lord about where the School of Navigation should go on outreach, I felt a burden for Thailand and specifically for the refugee crisis. This didn't make much sense to me initially, since we didn't need to sail a small boat to get there. But understanding came when I realized our calling was to reach people, not to sail boats. The boats were just a method of transportation to get to those in need, and there was a danger in taking our eyes off of that for the thrill of sailing. We had to keep reaching out to people wherever they were and however we could, until the only way to reach some on isolated islands was with small boats. This was a key mid-course correction in our ministry.

Two days later I brought together three other team members and asked them to pray with me about where we should go for outreach. I wanted to make sure this plan to minister among the refugees of former French Indochina was not just my own good idea. Three out of the four received direction that it should be Thailand or Southeast Asia. When I asked the Lord for confirmation, He led me to Revelation 7:14: "These are they who have come out of the great tribulation." That seemed to describe the refugees' situation quite accurately.

The following week I met with our handful of students to seek the Lord about where to go for outreach. Again, I didn't tell anyone what I felt. Nearly half received "Thailand." Another received "Matthew 5:3–16," which speaks of God blessing the poor and those who mourn as well as the challenge to let our light shine before men. The reference "Luke 10" came to my mind. This chapter tells of Jesus sending out the seventy with authority over the powers of darkness. I was encouraged by the hope of God doing the same through us.

I submitted this outreach possibility to Loren. He encouraged me to pursue it, mentioning that Gary Stephens, the School of Evangelism leader, was praying about bringing his students on outreach to Hong Kong to help with their refugee crisis. Gary and I arranged to go on a fact-finding trip to Hong Kong and Thailand starting in late October to see what ministry opportunities we might find. A Christian aid agency offered to sponsor us in Thailand, and I arranged to meet their field people there.

One evening, just before I left on the trip, our six-year-old daughter Lisa prayed during our family devotional time for the refugee children. Then she tugged on my arm. "Daddy, I want you to take my favorite doll to a little refugee girl who needs it." I got down on one knee, looked into her dark brown eyes and affirmed her generous heart as she handed me that prized doll.

"God knows the sacrifice you're making for some little girl. I know it will bring joy to her heart." I packed it carefully, knowing she had entrusted it to me with much love, and breathed a silent prayer. *Lord, help me find the right little one who needs the encouragement of this special doll.*

When we arrived in Hong Kong, Gary connected with the Jubilee Refugee Camp, where 8,100 refugees were squeezed into a facility built to house nine hundred. My heart ached as we visited whole families whose only home was a wooden bunk bed platform upon which they sat. Sanitation and electrical needs were enormous.

In Thailand we were given a tour by Joe and Colleen Harbison, a YWAM couple working among the Thai people. We also visited some projects in several refugee camps up north.

We learned more details of the refugee situation in Thailand. Cambodia had suffered from war and unrest for a long time. In the mid-1960s, during the Vietnam War, the Vietnamese used Cambodia as a staging ground for weapons and troops. This resulted in the pounding of U.S. bombing runs. In 1970 the Cambodian government head, Prince Sihanouk, was overthrown by the Premier Lon Nol. In 1975 Pol Pot, leader of the Khmer Rouge army, aligned with the Chinese communists, took control of Cambodia, and began to purge intellectuals in an attempt to produce a peasant society. Nearly two million perished during this reign of terror. In December 1978 Vietnam invaded Cambodia and put Hanoi-backed Heng Samrin in as president. Now in 1979 battles raged between the Vietnamese, the Khmer Rouge, and various Free Khmer groups for control of the country.

People fled the war, devastation, disease, and starvation in Cambodia (and Vietnam) by the tens of thousands, crossing over into Thailand to seek help. Once they crossed a border, they were classified as "refugees" and were able to receive aid from the international community overseen by the United Nations High Commission for Refugees (UNHCR).

On Saturday, November 3, we visited Sakaeo, a camp for Khmer Rouge refugees from Cambodia that had opened just a week and a half earlier. It was set up in former rice paddies, some forty miles from the Thailand–Cambodia border. I assumed they moved that far inland to avoid soldiers using the camp as a staging ground for border attacks.

When we arrived, the UN field officer took us into the camp to visit the various projects. We passed the "unaccompanied minors" section, housing children without families. Since the UN didn't know if their parents we alive or dead, they didn't call them orphans. The field officer said they planned to set up a communication post to unite children with any living relatives they could find. From there we walked to four hospital tents, which looked like small circus tents with no sides. Inside were hundreds of sick or dying refugees lying on grass mats. IV bottles hung from ropes tied between the tent poles, rehydrating the weak, malnourished, and deathly ill. We heard that roughly forty refugees died in the camp every day. Many were buried in mass graves.

We stepped around a dead body that had been dragged out of a hospital tent to wait for the burial crew. As I stood next to that dead body, deeply troubled in my spirit, a young boy looking about nine years of age took my hand and tried to communicate with me. He may have been thirteen or fourteen, but after four years of intense suffering and malnutrition, the children's ages were impossible to guess. I got down on one knee. "Do you speak English?"

He mumbled something in Khmer.

So I tried French. "*Parles-tu le français?*"

Again something muttered in Khmer.

I smiled and he grinned back. "God loves you, and I do too," I said in English. As he spoke to me in Khmer, we both smiled, sharing a warm, simple moment in the midst of the death and devastation around us.

When our guide began the tour again, the Khmer boy held my hand tightly as we continued to walk together. About thirty minutes after entering the camp, we arrived back at the entrance. The young boy pointed to the "unaccompanied minors" section and walked in that direction. I waved good-bye and went out the gate.

Our taxi driver, like many Thais, was eager to find out what was happening in this new refugee camp. During the ride back to Bangkok, we told him as much as we could about it.

In the middle of the night I woke from a deep sleep, shaking from sobs that racked my body. My heart hurt for the suffering children, especially for that young boy. I felt the Lord expressing His grief and pain through me as I wept. His heart was broken by this suffering. As I prayed for those refugees, I sensed the Lord say to me, "I want you working in the camps to express My heart. It doesn't matter so much what job you do; I want you there so My light can shine through you into that darkness. The more intense the darkness, the more obvious and bright your light will be." I fell back to sleep praying for the spiritual darkness over the Sakaeo camp and for the little boy who had seen the light of Jesus shine earlier that day.

The next morning Joe Harbison and I went to the Lumpini Transit Camp housed in a prison facility in Bangkok. This camp was for refugees hoping to be resettled in a third country like the United States, Canada, or France. Since we didn't know anyone, Joe and I just prayed, walked up to the huge steel gate like we belonged there, and knocked. A guard opened it and waved us through, probably thinking we were relief workers. In a huge open-air compound a young Vietnamese man approached us. When we told him we were Christians, he smiled and said, "Come, I want you to meet a friend of mine. He's a Christian leader here."

We walked into a huge warehouse-like building, crammed with hundreds of people, all living on mats carefully organized in rows on the cement floor. He led us to a man and his family, sitting on two or three mats with several children, surrounded by neatly arranged belongings. That was all they had for a home. The man invited us to sit down.

As I began to take a seat on his mat, a scripture poured through my mind. "I was in prison and you came to visit me. . . . Whatever you did for one of the least of these brothers of mine, you did for me" (Matt. 25:36, 40). A lump grew in my throat and tears pooled in my eyes before I was seated. I sensed God's heart for this precious family.

"Why have you come?" the man asked.

"The Lord knows that you are here and sent us to visit you. He loves you and will see you through this struggle. Keep trusting Him," I said. We talked for about half an hour. As we prepared to leave, I asked, "Can we pray for you?"

"Wait until I get all my children," he replied, gathering nine children and his wife.

After praying, I thought of Lisa's doll. They had a little girl about her age. I reached into my pack and took out the doll I had carried every day since I left Kona. "This is from my daughter," I said, handing it to the little girl. "She has been praying for you." What a joy it was to see the smile on his daughter's tiny face as she squeezed the doll to her cheek. Before leaving I took a photo of her to bring to Lisa.

The experience of that trip deeply etched a commissioning into my heart. We were called to visit those in prison and those in great difficulty, doing it as unto Jesus.

Heading back to Kona, I understood a little in my heart of what God felt for the refugees. I was determined to return with my team.

People from several YWAM centers around the world as well as the Crossroads DTS in Kona heard about our team going to the refugees in Thailand. Several approached me about working with us. In prayer we felt the Lord confirm each one.

Near the end of November, Joe Harbison, the YWAM leader in Thailand, called and told me he found an opening for us. We could develop a feeding center in the Khao-I-Dang camp, which had just opened on the Thailand–Cambodia border. This housed many of the Khmer Serei refugees (the Free Khmer) who had been fighting the Khmer Rouge and the Vietnamese. I sensed the Lord confirm our accepting this invitation, telling us to "Stand in the gap."

As our team prayed about this invitation, God encouraged us through several scriptures. They spoke about God's protection over us as well as challenging us to be an example to people while they observed our lives (1 Tim. 4:12). As the Lord took care of us, our job was to reveal Him to the people with our actions and attitudes more than with our words.

We heard there was still occasional artillery shelling of the camps. The Lord challenged me with the question, *Am I willing to lay down my life for His sake while working on the edge of the war?* Agonizing over this at supper that night, I quietly looked from Judi to my children, struggling over what they would go through if I never returned from Thailand. After wrestling with these thoughts for several days and nights, I finally yielded to the Lord and said, "Yes, Lord, regardless of what happens, I'm going." I decided that if the Lord required my life, I wanted to put my house in order before I left Kona. To do that, I needed to write a personal letter to Judi and each child about my hopes and aspirations for their future.

One evening I shared with Loren those thoughts and asked him to pray with me, seeking the Lord for a word about what He might require. As we prayed, Loren opened his Bible and began reading. A smile broke out on his face. "I sensed to read Psalm 91," he said. "Verse 16 says, 'With long life will I satisfy him and show him my salvation.' I think you will be fine." That promise lifted my spirits and would carry me through the following year when I found myself in dangerous situations. I was relieved. I no longer felt the need to write those letters to my family.

At the beginning of December, Todd Burke visited Kona. Having been a missionary to Phnom Penh, Cambodia, before its fall in 1975, he had just been looking in the Khao-I-Dang camp for any surviving friends. Instead he found nearly two hundred Christians from another body of believers, around twenty families that had escaped together with three of their church elders. We were thrilled, because we wanted the demonstration of Jesus in the camp to be seen as a local Khmer expression, not a foreign implant. We asked the Lord to work through these Christians to draw many others to Him.

During our prayer times in preparation for this trip, God directed us with other scriptures. Isaiah 58:6–12 showed us that God's chosen fast included dividing our bread with the hungry, bringing the homeless poor into the house, clothing the naked, and meeting the needs of the afflicted. Proverbs 24:11–12 challenged us with our personal responsibility to help those in need. "Rescue those being led away to death; hold back those staggering toward slaughter. If you say, 'But we knew nothing about this,' does not he who weighs the heart perceive it? Does not he who guards your life know it? Will he not repay each person according to what he has done?"

On December 6 we received news that our sponsoring agency in Thailand had withdrawn the invitation, saying they had enough workers in the camps and didn't need any more. I thought of that night in Thailand when I woke up weeping. God wanted His light to shine in those camps through us. I invited Bruce, one of the other leaders at the Kona campus, to pray with me about what to do and whether we should cancel the team to Thailand or move forward without the invitation. An awareness that the team should move forward filled my mind. I felt the Lord lead me to Genesis 17, where God confirmed His covenant with Abraham to make him the father of many nations. "Abraham . . . laughed and said to himself, 'Will a son be born to a man a hundred years old? Will Sarah bear a child at the age of ninety?' And Abraham said to God, 'If only Ishmael might live under your blessing!'" (Gen. 17:17–18). God encouraged Abraham, saying He would bless Ishmael, and then declared, "But my covenant I establish with Isaac, whom Sarah will bear to you by this time next year" (17:21).

Understanding exploded within me. The Lord was telling me that our attempt to begin a refugee ministry in Thailand through another agency was like trying to get our inheritance through an "Ishmael." God would bless them, but we were to move ahead and birth an "Isaac," our own YWAM ministry, and it would be established within a year. Excitement filled my mind. God wanted us to take the next twelve months to establish YWAM's own ministry to refugees. I prayed, trusting God to raise up someone to continue this process after the end of our three-month outreach.

Bruce said he felt the Lord direct him to read Jeremiah 31:13–25. These verses spoke of God comforting His people, refreshing them, and rewarding their work. Bruce encouraged us to continue the work. "God has plans for you with the refugees. Hang in there." So we pursued the doors God was opening to us.

On December 17, 1979, I prayed over Judi and our children. Lisa was now in elementary school, Joey was in preschool, and Daniel was one year old. I kissed each of them good-bye and departed with our team for the three-month outreach, wondering what kinds of adventures and challenges God had for us in Thailand.

TWENTY-FOUR

Refugee Camps

OUR plan was to live near the Khao-I-Dang (KID) refugee camp in the small border town of Aranyaprathet, 150 miles east of Bangkok. With the help of Joe Harbison, we spent our first few days in the big city getting supplies organized. Joe and his wife, Colleen, had been developing YWAM's ministry among the people of Thailand, but he graciously helped us start working with the Cambodian and Vietnamese refugees.

A second team, coming from Los Angeles with John and Jill Bills, was scheduled to arrive on December 25. I wanted to open the door for them to the Bangkok transit camps so they would have a ministry opportunity ready for them on Christmas day, when it's so hard to be separated from family. But as I tried to make contact with someone regarding the transit camp, I only found empty offices. Nothing seemed to work out.

On December 21, I realized it might take several more days to get an opening to the transit camps. Facing closed doors, I prayed, "Lord, what are You trying to say through this?" When I stopped to listen, I sensed Him telling me, "Go to Aranyaprathet."

"But, Lord, I have a team arriving in four days. I need to open a door to the transit camps for them. What am I supposed to do?"

"Go to Aranyaprathet," came the reply.

"But, Lord, the Los Angeles team," I groaned.

"Go to Aranyaprathet."

"Okay, if that really is You, please confirm it tonight when I pray with our whole team."

When the team returned to the little apartment where we were staying, I led the group in prayer, asking the Lord if we were all to go to Aranyaprathet the next day. Everyone received "Yes" in answer to prayer. I gulped and gave the directive to depart in the morning.

Joe Harbison drove us out that next day, December 22, in a green Toyota pickup truck with supplies stacked high around our team. Four hours brought us to a little dusty border town three miles from Cambodia, reminiscent of what I had seen in old black-and-white cowboy movies. Dirt roads stretched in several directions, all lined with unpainted wooden houses like two-story sheds.

After inviting God's blessing and spiritually cleansing our house, we spent the afternoon scouring our little place and chasing out the rats. We didn't have an extended prayer meeting or do any spiritual warfare; we just cleaned and moved in. During that process, the UN camp director for KID stopped by to welcome us. He handed me a paper with instructions on how to evacuate the border area in case the war—three miles away—spilled over into Thailand.

"There's nothing to worry about. This is only in case of an emergency," he assured me. I thanked him and offered to meet him in the camp the next day.

The downstairs of our house was an open garage area with an accordion-style sliding metal gate that secured the inside. We found a squatty potty at the back with a cooking area just in front of it. The cooking equipment was a clay pot with charcoal and a wok to place on top of it when the fire was hot. Three simple rooms occupying the upstairs were divided by partitions that ended below the tin roof. Curtains replaced doors.

Joe and I would return to Bangkok in two days to welcome the Los Angeles team, so he and I slept on the floor of the downstairs garage next to some large boxes of food supplies. About midnight I woke up to Joe knocking against me, yelling and kicking off his sleeping bag. A rat sat on his knee, trying to gnaw into one of the boxes of food. With our flashlights, we illuminated a dozen ravenous rats scurrying around, some with open sores on their backs. We both retreated to the top of the picnic table set up for our team meals, and that's where we spent that fitful night.

The next morning, Joe and I drove to the KID camp on a road that paralleled the border. Located six or seven miles from the Thailand–Cambodia border, the camp spread out like a sprawling village of bamboo- and thatch-roofed shacks, surrounded by a tall barbed wire fence. After the machine-gun-carrying Thai military admitted us through the gate, we met with a Khmer-speaking former missionary to Cambodia who was working as a translator for the UN.

"How are the two hundred Christians doing that came into the camp in early December?" I asked.

"They're doing well, but more Christians are now in the camp."

"Did more church groups come in?" I asked.

"No," he replied with a broad smile. "The refugees saw something different on the faces of the original two hundred Christians. So they asked, 'Where did you find that peace? We've seen our families murdered and our Buddhist priests executed. Nothing we trusted in saved them. What do you have?' Then the Christians told them about Jesus. Now the church group has grown to over eight hundred."

"Praise God! That's exciting," I said.

Next I met with the UN camp director about the feeding center we had been invited to establish in Section 13. He informed me they were not yet ready to put refugees in that section. So I visited other projects in the camp, asking if they needed additional help. Most said yes. In the thick of this intense crisis, people were overworked and projects under-staffed. I soon had places for all of our team to work.

The next morning, December 24, I set up a rotating schedule. Half the team stayed at the house to intercede and the other half went to the camp. The following day they would switch. This was like what

Nehemiah did (in 4:13–18) when the enemy tried to keep the people from rebuilding the walls of Jerusalem. He stationed some to stand in the unprotected places while others worked. I believed prayer support was critical to our daily work with the refugees.

After getting everyone situated, I took the four-hour bus ride back to Bangkok to meet the team arriving at the airport on Christmas Day. All the way I thought, *Lord, what was the hurry? The UN wasn't ready for us to open our feeding center. Why the rush?*

Back in Bangkok on Christmas Day I went to the post office to make a phone call to Judi and our children. I wished them all a merry Christmas and told them how much I missed them and loved them. Judi assured me they were all doing well in spite of the fact that I wasn't there. I felt at peace in the midst of my loneliness. This was the first Christmas I wasn't with my family.

The Los Angeles team arrived later that morning, excited to be in Thailand even though it was Christmas. They felt the Lord ask them to take two weeks to pray before beginning work in the transit camps, so they didn't need me and I returned to Aranyaprathet. The thought kept plaguing me, *Why the hurry to get to Aranyaprathet three days ago?*

Two of our girls began working with a clinic for malnourished infants. Because the mothers were dying of starvation, they could not nurse their babies. Most of the dying infants could no longer assimilate food, as their digestive systems shut down. Our girls tried putting a small amount of formula in a Chinese porcelain rice spoon, and letting the liquid run down the short grooved handle into the baby's mouth. Almost always it would come right back up. Our girls silently took authority over the enemy, who wanted to "kill, steal, and destroy." They kept offering food and soon the babies were able to absorb nourishment.

Within a week, two of the refugee translators working at the clinic asked our students why they came to the camp and how they got the babies to respond. They shared their testimonies and explained how prayer had helped the babies. In a short time these two translators yielded their hearts to Jesus.

Soon field leaders from various organizations began asking me, "Do you have a construction worker?" "Do you have a nurse?" "Do you have a doctor available?" Everywhere I turned, field agencies needed workers even though their main offices in the States were likely saying, "No, thank you, we don't need your help. We have more workers than we need." I was grateful that YWAM was field-led, not headquarters-led. That allowed versatility and the ability to respond quickly when emergencies arose. God continually encouraged us to be in the camps, letting His light shine through us. If a worker was willing to do any task, the doors were open.

In one of our daily prayer times during the first few days there, the Lord led us to review Isaiah 58. We saw God's priority in a four-fold commissioning to us: (1) feed the hungry, (2) provide homes for the homeless, (3) clothe the naked, and (4) meet the needs of the afflicted. Starving refugees desperately needed food. A home provided a sense of security and peace. Clothing provided a sense of human dignity to people created in the image of God. Ministering to the afflicted included helping those with medical needs. Meeting these practical needs allowed God's light to shine through us.

When new opportunities opened, we would ask, "Does it fit into Isaiah 58? Will it bring us into direct contact with people? Will it give opportunity for the light of Jesus to shine through us?" If the answer to these three questions was yes and Jesus confirmed it to us, we would pursue it.

Two weeks after our arrival, the number of believers in the camp grew to over two thousand. People said, "If only we had heard this good news in Cambodia, we would have believed. But nobody told us." Several said, "I have to return to Cambodia to tell this message." We were able to bring quantities of Bibles into the camp. One refugee took as many Bibles as he could carry and crossed the border back into Cambodia to bring this good news to his people.

Amazingly, by mid-January 1980 the number of believers in the camp grew to over twenty thousand. At night many small groups all across the camp met around a Bible and a kerosene lantern. Though they were refused building materials to construct a church, many brought bamboo and thatching from their own homes to form a structure for prayer and worship.

Also in January the YWAM director from Amsterdam, Holland, called me to say a medical team with a doctor and several nurses had prepared to come to Thailand with a Dutch mission. At the last minute the Dutch mission had backed out, and now he had a medical team ready to go.

"We don't have a medical work in the camp right now," I said. "But let me pray about it, look into options, and I'll call you back in a day or two."

"Please don't wait too long," he said. "They already have tickets to arrive on January 19."

Though we had no options ourselves, I sensed God affirm that we should tell them to come and accept them as our workers. I called back and gave them the okay.

On January 16, Loren briefly came to Bangkok and preached a message to our staff from Mark 6. In the feeding of the five thousand, he explained, Jesus had compassion on the crowd spiritually and physically. Afterward, when Jesus sent the disciples ahead of Him across the lake, Jesus came walking on the water. Verses 51–52 say, "They were completely amazed, for they had not understood about the loaves; their hearts were hardened." Loren encouraged us to keep a servant's attitude and ask God for understanding as He opened doors for us or closed others. We took Loren's message to heart and continually asked the Lord to give us understanding as we faced the various challenges in establishing the ministry.

Two days later at the regular UN Coordinating Committee meeting for all relief agencies, we were told that they were closing an outpatient medical clinic in Section 2 of the Khao-I-Dang camp, the current agency having withdrawn. They asked if anyone had a medical team to take it over. When no one responded, I sheepishly raised my hand and said, "We have a medical team arriving tomorrow. We can take it over." I thanked God that before the medical team arrived, He had already provided the doorway of opportunity for them.

This happened regularly as teams and individuals contacted us about coming to serve in Thailand. When God said "yes" about accepting a new worker or team, a door of service would open. We soon ran a medical clinic, a postoperative hospital ward, a feeding center, a vocational center, a school for children, a distribution center for clothing and sandals, and many other projects.

As a rule of thumb I based the rightness of a team or person coming on the word of the Lord, not the availability of work. We could have told teams to wait until we firmly established the work. But each time the Lord confirmed the rightness of a team coming, a door of service would open. As I thought about this later, I realized that God wanted to quickly grow a refugee ministry and establish YWAM as a mission for this type of ministry. Our saying "no" to a team would have cut off a part of our mission that wanted to join the new thrust. God was entrusting us with a major responsibility.

On January 22, I attended a political briefing arranged by a retired U.S. Air Force colonel who was working with us. The focus was the Thailand–Cambodia border, where our team was located. Standing before a conference table, the speaker began, "Last month we observed a massive buildup of troops along the border above and below Aranyaprathet. We concluded that they planned to cross over and attack the town, so we notified the Thai military to prepare for a possible attack on December 22. For some strange reason, the troops didn't attack; they just dissipated. About a week later they gathered in the same way. Once again we notified the Thai military, and a couple of days later the troops dispersed. We don't know what they intend to do now."

Although those giving the briefing were confused, I had clear understanding. I now knew why God wanted us in Aranyaprathet on December 22. He was asking us literally to stand in the gap by our physical presence on behalf of the people we were called to serve. As He protected us, He protected them. Later I found confirmation in Jeremiah 29:7: "Seek the peace and prosperity of the city to which I have carried you into exile. Pray to the LORD for it, because if it prospers, you too will prosper." We didn't pray or do any specific spiritual warfare on December 22; we just cleaned and moved into our house. But our physical presence was a spiritual warfare on behalf of the people we were called to.

We concluded that if anything happened to any of our workers serving at the border zone, it would not be an accident in God's eyes. So we required anyone working with us at the border to put in writing what their guidance from God was for serving there. That way, if something happened to a worker, we could communicate to loved ones his or her divine direction, that the person's life was an investment on behalf of the refugees and God's kingdom. Because one young man who felt called to serve on the border was under eighteen, we asked his parents to write a letter of affirmation to that call. I was moved as I read the commitment of his parents as they released their son into the purposes and protection of God.

Knowing well the dangers of our work, we began our days with singing and praise. Often I would sense a heaviness lift off my shoulders during those times. I began to see worship as an act of spiritual warfare. It would drive the enemy away, because he wasn't comfortable to stay around praise and worship to God.

In late February persecution against the Christians developed in the camp. Roving bands of thugs attacked the evening Bible studies and beat the people. One day a mob tried to drag one of the church leaders outside the camp, intending to kill him. Our team ran for the UN camp director, who came and rescued him. Fearing for their lives, many abandoned the church. The Christians dropped from twenty thousand to seven thousand. Though this was a major setback, we rejoiced with the thousands who, refined by fire, stood their ground against this opposition and refused to turn back. Over the coming months the number of gathered believers built up again to over 28,000. And with God's protection, we never lost a worker.

My team and I began to sense that if a YWAM relief service was to be established in Thailand, our time there could not be for just a three-month school outreach. We believed God was calling several of us to stay on for the rest of the year, and some for even longer. I sensed the Lord ask me to stay for one year. So I called Judi in Hawaii and invited her to join me in praying about this, understanding that if God confirmed that direction, she and the children would join me in April for the rest of the year. Team members communicated with family and sought God over several weeks. In the end most of the team felt God leading them to stay longer. Several from the ministry would still be serving in Thailand three decades later.

TWENTY-FIVE

Multiplying Compassion

WE SOON had over seventy workers serving in five refugee camps. With Judi and our children coming to join me in Thailand in two months, I moved to Bangkok, turning the work in Aranyaprathet over to Steve and Marie Goode, a couple who had joined us from Lausanne, Switzerland. Being in Bangkok made it easier for me to manage the team arrivals and departures and our relationships with the UN and the Thai military. Running errands in town, I would often zip back and forth between various offices by *tuk tuk*, a three-wheeled rickshaw-type motorcycle taxi, not for the faint of heart. They were one-third the price of regular taxis, but three times the danger. Precariously, they carried people next to the large spinning wheels of massive buses and huge transport trucks, while we breathed in sooty clouds of black exhaust from those behemoths.

Since the team in Aranyaprathet had grown so large, we had to rent two more houses. We "showered" by scooping water from huge clay pots. None of these pots had covers, so mosquitoes bred rapidly. This resulted in a dengue fever epidemic sweeping through our team. I went out to spend time with the team in early March and also came down with dengue fever. Once the clay pots were cleaned and covers were put over them, the epidemic ended.

I lay in bed in Aranyaprathet for over a week until I had enough strength to make the four-hour bus trip back to Bangkok. But even back in the big city, I could not regain my strength. With a high fever and an inability to adequately take in liquids, my electrolyte levels got out of balance. My mind was dizzy, cloudy, and confused. I could barely lift my head off my pillow. A doctor lived next door, and the team carried me to him several times. Because he didn't have the supplies to give me an IV at his home, the doctor would inject a vein in my arm with a large syringe of saline solution. This gave me instant strength and clarity so I could walk home. But half an hour later I was once again flat on my back in bed with a terrible headache and a cloudy mind.

A year later I learned that a YWAM staff member from South Africa, on board the Mercy Ship M/V *Anastasis* in Greece, woke up the night of March 13, 1980, with a vision of my face and the Lord saying to her, "Bad health." She interceded for me that night, which was when I was at my weakest.

My struggle with dengue continued until mid-April when Judi and our children arrived. They boosted my morale. As a family we went for a week to the Juniper Tree, a missionary retreat center at Hua Hin, a seaside town south of Bangkok. Finally, I found myself reviving.

On Saturdays in Bangkok I loved taking Judi and our three children to the Dusit Zoo. Each child had a favorite animal, but they all enjoyed watching the three mongooses. Because we had mongooses in Hawaii, they were very familiar to the children when everything else was so strange. My bedtime stories with the kids revolved around Herman the mongoose. I told them, "If Herman is okay spending time with his two cousins at the Dusit Zoo, then you'll be okay spending time in Thailand while Daddy works with the refugees." And they were.

In addition to the Khao-I-Dang camp (which by late January had closed to new arrivals), there were unofficial camps along the border just inside Cambodia, where thousands more gathered, unable to cross into Thailand. The UN didn't consider them refugees. To have that status they had to cross a border. Those still in Cambodia were considered "internally displaced persons." At the end of April we asked the Lord if, along with our other activities, we should attempt to get involved in those border camps, and He directed us to do so. The 007 camp was one such place, a ramshackle collection of tents and huts inside the Cambodian border, across no man's land and a tank trap. Ox carts came and went, carrying rice, food, and other supplies to the interior of Cambodia. There was no official border post. People crossed at their own risk.

At the beginning of June, a visitor coming through Bangkok interviewed me for an article he would publish about YWAM's relief work. "How has God led you to develop this ministry?" he asked.

"From the beginning I asked the Lord to give me understanding of what He was doing," I responded. "I learned that if the Lord calls a group in, things come together for them. In the spring a group of twenty-one wanted to come from Switzerland. In prayer we sensed it was right, though we didn't have specific jobs for them. When they came, we found plenty for them to do. Within two weeks, we already needed more people. That's God's sense of humor. You see waves coming and think, *We'll never figure out how it's going to work,* and all of a sudden it does."

"What would you call that stage of ministry?" the interviewer asked.

"I see this first stage as the growing phase. The key word to me is *excitement.* Many people from our mission have come in, eager to reach out to the refugees."

"Are you still in that stage?"

"No. A couple of months ago the Lord led us into a stabilizing phase," I replied. "Here the key word is *commitment.* By the time the fourth wave of people came, the first was leaving and those who had led projects departed. This left two or three people as pillars, trying to hold up what seven or eight had done. We needed to move toward stability and commitment."

"Was that a difficult process?"

"No. In fact, I've never seen pioneering happen so fast. This is not because of what we've been doing. I believe it's because God is concerned for these refugees and these nations. I have to be careful not to slow down too much. We're adding long-term people committed to specific responsibilities. With this stability we can grow and receive more teams."

"Does that mean you will stop receiving new teams until things stabilize?"

"Absolutely not," I exclaimed. "New people keep the work alive and exciting by their enthusiasm, freshness, zeal, and hope. We need it."

"Do you think there will be another stage following this one?"

"Yes," I answered. "I believe we're already looking at the next one, the expansion phase. The key word is *multiplication*. To expand you need committed people keeping the present things going, and others with vision expanding into new ones. Don't sacrifice the present ministries for future vision. In other words, don't kill the mother while birthing a baby. Grow into it."

After the interview a thought entered my mind. *What did God tell Moses about driving the enemies out of the Promised Land so the children of Israel could possession it?* I found it in Exodus 23:29–30. God said, "But I will not drive them out in a single year, because the land would become desolate and the wild animals too numerous for you. Little by little I will drive them out before you, until you have increased enough to take possession of the land." That's how God was leading us.

In mid-June, before the rainy season made the dirt roads impassible, the UN and the Thai military organized a voluntary return to Cambodia. Each refugee was offered a repatriation kit, which included a hoe head, seeds, and a few hand tools and utensils to help them start life over again. The various agencies were asked to supply things for this project. We volunteered to provide some items for the kits, because another group had offered to fund them for us. But when we sent the bills to that group, they declined to cover those costs. This left us owing suppliers $9,000.

Being unable to pay these bills, we sought the Lord for understanding. He showed us that our anointing was not as a funding agency but as a people (operational) one. We were called to place our people where they could have personal contact with the recipients of our services, where our light could shine in the darkness. We were not to just throw money at a need. We confessed our presumption and asked God's forgiveness. Later another Christian organization offered to cover our part, but we didn't make that mistake again.

About five days after the voluntary repatriation, on June 23 the Vietnamese Army launched an attack across the border into Thailand, killing Thai soldiers, villagers, refugees, and Khmer troops. What had been avoided on December 22 at Aranyaprathet now touched the Mak Mun border camp north of us. When the shooting stopped a few days later, Steve Goode and I drove out to the camp to check on a group of Cambodians. As we drove along the border road, Thai tanks were lined up on their side of the road with Vietnamese tanks on the Cambodian side. Taking a deep breath, I prayed as Steve drove between the muzzles of the tank cannons pointing over our heads at each other. By the time we got to the camp, everyone had fled. We found some refugees wandering around in the open fields on the Thai side. We couldn't find our friends, and since the camp was still occupied by the invading army, we were advised not to enter it.

As Steve and I departed for home, three or four expatriate relief workers ignored the warning and went into the camp. In the newspaper the next day, we read that those workers had been kidnapped by the Vietnamese. It took about two weeks for them to be released. The evil and violence around us were a harsh reality. We had to trust in God for protection as we continued our relief work.

One morning while attending the UN Coordinating Committee meeting for all relief agencies, I overheard a startling conversation. A woman seated in the row in front of me blurted out to her neighbor rather sarcastically, "Yesterday a group of visitors came into the camp. As they saw the refugees, several of them began to weep. What a joke. They don't have a clue about these people." I no longer heard what the UN speaker was discussing. Sitting there lost in my own thoughts, I realized that all of us who came to work with the refugees arrived with preconceived ideas and false expectations. After seeing the media reports of the plight of the refugees, one of my preconceived ideas was "suffering equates innocence." Soon after arriving in Thailand I discovered this was not true. I had seen evil, treachery, and deception in the hearts of those suffering people.

I recalled what I had read on February 3 in *My Utmost for His Highest* by Oswald Chambers. "When a merely moral man or woman comes in contact with baseness and immorality and treachery, the recoil is so desperately offensive to human goodness that the heart shuts up in despair. The marvel of the Redemptive Reality of God is that the worst and the vilest can never get to the bottom of His love."

We had two choices. Seeing the corruption and evil, we could stop caring and harden our hearts like the woman in front of me. Or, adjusting to the reality of what we found, we could recognize that God called us to minister to the needy and suffering regardless of their moral state. Jesus knew what was in man (John 2:25), yet he could be moved with compassion (Mark 1:41).

My spirit ached as I prayed silently, *Lord, help me adjust my preconceived ideas to reality. Let me weep with the refugees when I leave here at the end of this year, just like I did when I arrived. Please don't let my heart be hardened.*

One of the projects proposed by the UN was feeding a starving population of Khmer Rouge women and children traveling with their soldier husbands near the border. Most agencies refused to touch it. Their funding sources would not allow them to help what they called "the Khmer Rouge cause." Sacks of rice intended for this group of family members would go back into Cambodia and be eaten by the soldiers, while the women and children were left starving.

I was glad when I heard about several Christian aid agencies who found a way to help these starving people. Instead of giving them bags of rice, which the soldiers would take, the agencies cooked hot meals at the border. The women and children came and ate there and then returned to their camp. This enabled the starving to receive the help they needed.

God, I realized, doesn't choose sides in conflicts. He's above them, trying to touch the hearts of people on both sides, urging reconciliation.

I so enjoyed my time in Thailand that I wanted to stay longer than my twelve-month commitment, which would end in December, just over two months away. I asked the Lord, "Did You really mean just one year when You spoke to me in February? Can't I stay for another year?" I received no response. I struggled, hoping to hear God confirm my desires to stay longer. But God had spoken earlier; I just didn't want to hear Him. He had told me in February that I was to serve in Thailand for twelve months. Though I kept persisting, I found no peace or clarity.

On October 8, I asked the Lord again, "Do we extend our time in Thailand?" I had the impression to begin my daily Bible reading. As I read Isaiah 28:18, it felt like the wind had been knocked out of me. "Your covenant with death will be annulled; your agreement with the grave will not stand." I immediately thought of Psalm 91:16, the scripture Loren had received for me before I had come to Thailand: "With long life I will satisfy him and show him my salvation." A realization crashed over me like a rogue wave of the sea. I could stay beyond the twelve months, but God's promise of protection was for one year. After that point my contract for protection would be canceled. I immediately responded to God. I arranged our flight to depart on December 17, exactly one year to the day from the date I flew from Hawaii to Thailand. I wasn't going to take any chances.

Steve and Marie Goode and John and Jill Bills threw a small party with a birthday cake in early December 1980 to celebrate with Judi and me the birth of YWAM Relief Services Thailand. We had seen the fulfillment of Genesis 17:21, the birthing of our "Isaac" within twelve months.

As we approached the end of my tenure, I arranged to have an outside accountant audit our financial records so I could turn over a clean slate to Steve, who was to take over as director a week before we departed. At that time Thailand was a cash-based economy, with no checks or credit cards, especially in the open market. Almost never was I offered a receipt for a purchase. Eventually we had several people making purchases for our work, as we managed feeding programs, medical programs, occupational and vocational programs, clothing programs, language learning programs, and more. We told them to write out their own receipts if no receipt was offered, and have the seller initial it.

Unfortunately, as the accountant checked our books, he found nearly $1,750 not accounted for with receipts or records. When I asked the Lord what to do, I sensed Him say to me, "Give and trust Me." I was in the process of arranging the airline tickets for my family, so I had about $1,800 in hand. Talking this over with Steve, I put $1,750 of my cash into the ministry account, telling the Lord I trusted Him to provide for my family. A few days before we were to fly out, we were still unable to pay for our tickets. Steve mentioned to our teams that we had a financial need, and within a couple of hours the full amount we needed came in. I thanked the Lord for His help and for the way He had underlined the practical application of the truth that as the leader I carried the financial responsibility for the work.

En route to Hawaii on December 17, I reflected on all I had seen over the past year. When I took our first team to Thailand the previous December, I saw the devastation of war and asked God, "Why?" I slowly began to see one positive result of this horrible violence. Cambodia had been a very hard soil spiritually. When missionaries first went there, the people refused their message, threw stones at them, and drove them out of their villages. Then trouble came upon the nation, and hundreds of people came to the Lord before Phnom Penh fell to the Khmer Rouge in 1975. After this the borders were closed, and for four years no one heard anything from Cambodia.

In December 1979 thousands fled across the border and revealed the atrocities. Khmer Rouge dictator Pol Pot had especially targeted the intellectuals in his attempt to establish an agrarian society in Cambodia. His violent campaign led to the deaths of nearly two million of his own people. Seeing the Christians grow from two hundred to multiple thousands in the Khao-I-Dang camp in such a short time following their arrival, I recognized a spiritually fertile soil. Having been uprooted from family, culture, nation, and religion, the people were open and searching for answers.

But that openness lasted only a year. In December 1980, during my last visit to the camp, I saw the first spirit houses put up in Khao-I-Dang. Those who hadn't responded to the gospel had returned to the old ways. The period of openness to the gospel was only a short window of time in that nation. I realized that as a mission we needed to respond quickly and run to nations in crisis when we heard God's call.

Life Out of Death

AFTER that year in Thailand, I was invited to move aboard YWAM's Mercy Ship, the M/V *Anastasis*. Judi and I and our three children joined the ship just outside Athens, Greece, in February 1981, while it was being refitted in Elefsis Harbor near Piraeus. A special treat was finding Don and Evey Heckman on board. We hadn't worked together since the first Sahara trip in 1975.

One day as I sat for a meal with my family at a circular table in the ship's forward dining hall, Don Heckman came by.

"Did you hear they closed the YWAM center in M'Pouto?" he asked.

"What? That can't be," I gasped. "Who told you that? How do you know?"

"I have a memo that was sent out about it. Didn't you see it?"

"No," I replied numbly.

"I'll go get you my copy," Don offered.

I looked at Judi. "After all that has happened, how can this be? Maybe it's a mistake."

"Joe, you just have to trust the Lord," Judi reassured me. "We did what God told us to do. That's all we're responsible for."

In a few minutes Don returned and handed me a three-page memo. My name was on the list of recipients at the top, but my copy never reached me. I stared in disbelief as I read, "It is with great reluctance and sadness of heart that we close this base. . . . We do not know why, with the fruit that we see, the Lord is not permitting us to continue in West Africa at this time. The last leader had to return to Europe due to hepatitis, which not only afflicted him but his wife and child too. At that time they were the only ones at the base in M'Pouto." The memo went on to explain that the two houses had been returned to their owners and the center was now closed. And with that, my vision for French West Africa died. *How could things end up this way? Where are You, Lord?*

Understanding of why God let the base in M'Pouto close came slowly. In the fall Judi and I traveled to YWAM's training school in Le Gault-la-Forêt, France, which Daniel and Maguy Schaerer directed. Although I had been to the center before, this was my first time teaching there. Early in the week, two young men on staff, who had been on the team that closed down the center in Ivory Coast, challenged me. "Why did you let the base in M'Pouto get shut down? Couldn't you have done something? Why didn't God give us victory?"

Silently asking God to help me answer these questions, I responded, "Actually, I didn't know it was being closed down until after the fact. Like you, I've asked the Lord many times, 'Why did You let that happen?' I didn't get any easy answers. Instead I was reminded of the stories of the early missionaries who went to West Africa in the 1800s. They packed their clothes in coffins to sail to that continent. Many died during their first year there. Death was a part of the price for establishing those first mission posts. I sensed the Lord saying to me, 'You have entered into the flow of history for this part of the world.' Why should we expect less of a challenge in pioneering YWAM's first center in French West Africa?" After this conversation I realized that God was in control of the ministry in West Africa, even if we faced challenges and setbacks for which we didn't have answers.

I enjoyed teaching in French again, and seeing people equipped to join the mission to reach the French world encouraged me tremendously. Judi and I returned to the ship with renewed hope.

Working with the ship's DTS, we prayed for the Polish refugees who had just been stranded in Austria when Poland closed its borders. The oppressive government of Poland imposed martial law to stamp out political opposition. Many people were arrested, and some were killed. Seeking the Lord about where to go on outreach at the end of the three-month lecture phase, we sensed direction to work with the refugees in Austria. In early January 1982 we arrived just outside Vienna to work for two months teaching English and cultural orientation classes. By the end of that time, fourteen Polish people had yielded their hearts to the Lord.

Many of the refugees we met worried about the families they had left behind in Poland; they had received no news. This opened up a new ministry opportunity. John, a staff member in Austria, and I decided that we would go to Poland, in spite of the closed borders, to carry news to the family members, locate some of our Christian friends, and assess the spiritual needs in the country. We attempted to get visas in Austria, but they were denied. So I returned to Greece, carrying John's passport, and requested visas at the Polish Embassy in Athens, and they were granted. The ship leaders prayed over me before I returned to Austria, asking that we would be like Joshua and Caleb, who went into the Promised Land with the twelve spies, saw beyond the giants to the good fruit, and brought back a positive report. "Release them in the gifts of the Spirit. Lead them to specific people. May they hear the voice of the Lord clearly and see God's purposes for this trip accomplished. May their words bring encouragement and healing to those who are suffering."

Back in Austria in late April, John and I boarded a train to Poland. The border guards didn't want to let us in, but because we had legitimate visas, they admitted us. We traveled to Krakow. Moving into a hotel that likely had eavesdropping microphones hidden in the rooms, we unpacked and prepared to find a friend of John's in the city. Since this was during the communist era, Christians were sorely persecuted. We carried no addresses in writing to avoid implicating anyone if we were searched. John had memorized the contact information of the friend he had previously visited. When the taxi stopped in front of a house, John gasped, "Don't stop. This is not the right place. It should be an apartment building."

We returned to our hotel, and I asked John what he remembered from his previous visit.

"Well, I was met at the airport, and we traveled by bus to a major road that circled the city. We got off the bus and then caught another bus that brought us to the neighborhood where my friend lived."

"Let's look at the city map. Maybe we can figure out something from that."

Looking at our map, we saw that our hotel was on the road coming from the airport. And looking out our hotel room window, we saw a major cross street with a bus stop on the corner.

"That bus stop might be where we transferred from the airport bus. But I can't really be sure. Let's go down and try to catch a bus," John suggested.

Waiting at the bus stop, we watched buses from two different routes come and go. When the next bus arrived from a third route, John said, "Okay, let's get on." The bus passed several stops, then turned off the main road and into a residential area. "Quick, let's get off. None of this looks familiar," John whispered.

Standing at a cross street, I had the thought come to mind. *Turn right.* I was afraid to say anything. It seemed too weird. But, pointing right, I asked, "Does anything look familiar?"

"Not really," he replied.

I started walking toward the right anyway, and John walked with me. At the end of the street we arrived at a T-junction. Stopping at that inter-section, I had an inner impression. *Look left.* Pointing to the left, I asked John, "Does anything look familiar to you over there?" Ahead, a huge, gray cement apartment complex loomed, nearly filling a city block.

"Well, no, I can't be sure. The previous time I came here at night."

I didn't tell John what I sensed. *Maybe that impression wasn't anything.* We took the left fork and continued to walk. After wandering for half an hour, we gave up. Then I finally told John about the impressions I had.

Another thought came to mind. "Duncan Campbell and Loren talked about the principle of the ax head," I said. "In 2 Kings 6:1–7 Elisha and the company of the prophets went down to the Jordan River to cut poles. As one of the prophets chopped a tree, his ax head fell into the water. He asked Elisha to help him find it. When shown where it fell in, Elisha made the ax head float and retrieved it."

"I know the story," John responded. "But what does that have to do with us?"

"Well," I began, "the principle they associated with that story is, when you are following the Lord's direction and you lose your way, don't keep struggling in your predicament. Go back to the last thing you heard the Lord say to you clearly and pick up the thread again there."

"How do we do that?" John asked.

"Let's go back to the place I sensed that last impression, before I ignored it and we wandered around in circles." We walked back to the T-junction. I prayed, "Lord, please forgive me for my insensitivity, ignoring what might have been Your direction and just wandering off on my own." Then I said to John, "Look left. Does anything look familiar to you?"

"If that complex is the right place, then it would be that middle door," John said, pointing.

We walked over to the entryway of the complex, went through that door, and looked at the names listed by the stairwell. One listing had the same first name as the person we were searching for, so we hesitantly walked up the stairs to the second floor and sheepishly knocked on the door of the apartment.

The door swung open. A woman smiled and said, "John, I'm so glad to see you. I've been praying that God would send you here. In this difficult time we asked the Lord to send us help." Astonished, I tried to regain composure as John introduced me to his friend. She welcomed us in and then invited some of her Christian friends to come over to meet us. The Lord gave us words of encouragement for them. This experience opened the door to many years of ministry touching the lives of that fellowship and thousands more in Poland.

As I returned to Greece, I thought about how this miracle in Poland didn't happen because I had great faith. Rather, when I was in a difficult circumstance and had no other option but to call upon God for help, He graciously answered and worked the miraculous. I realized that God responds to our struggles in this way, not because we are so special, but because we so desperately need His help to accomplish His purposes.

AT THE end of December 1982 my family and I returned to Kona. I sensed the Lord put a new choice before me. I could either keep pioneering new places (maybe another five or six more in my lifetime) or train many others to pioneer hundreds of new places. I chose multiplication, to train others, instead of just finding personal fulfillment in what I could pioneer.

Within three years I began serving as the associate dean of the College of Christian Ministries (CCM) in YWAM's newly developing University of the Nations (U of N). Judi served with me, arranging events for the CCM degree students at the Kona campus. At times the enemy discouraged me with the thought that I was like an old war horse put out to pasture. But I threw off that thought when I saw the excitement and enthusiasm in the eyes of the students being trained.

Occasionally I had the opportunity to return to the French world and see for myself all that God was doing. From time to time I taught in YWAM schools in Lausanne, Switzerland; Le Gault-la-Forêt, France; and Quebec, Canada. A second French center eventually opened in Saint-Paul-Trois-Chateaux, Provence, as a springboard to the French-speaking world. Patricia Wolf, a fourteen-year-old sponsored by Daniel Schaerer in our 1973 Paris outreach and a student in the first DTS at Le Gault-la-Forêt in 1978, eventually began an orphanage in Thailand and, years later, another in a nearby country.

In 1982 YWAM French Ministries sponsored the first Summer of Service in French West Africa like I had done in Paris in 1973. Over 120 Europeans came down, joined by 120 Africans, to witness to their faith in Burkina Faso. They saw many conversions. A young Burkinabe from a Muslim family, Noufou Kangambega, heard the enthusiasm of these young people over a radio station. Going to a public auditorium, he watched a dramatic presentation of the gospel. Through it he understood who Jesus was, why Jesus came, and what the spiritual condition of his own life was. He surrendered his heart to the Lord that night and went on to become the director of YWAM in Burkina Faso.

Gradually, French YWAMers reached into a growing number of countries in the French world and beyond.

TWENTY-SEVEN

God's Faithfulness

IN JULY 1988, I had the opportunity to see what God was doing in the French world again when I returned to Le Gault-la-Forêt, France. Daniel Schaerer, who had taken responsibility for coordinating YWAM's work among the French-speaking countries of the world, had organized a strategy conference focusing on French West Africa. I came from Hawaii, and more than twenty other YWAM leaders came from French-speaking Europe and French West Africa to plan how to establish Christian ministries in all twenty-seven French-speaking countries and island nations around Africa.

On Sunday morning I climbed three flights of stairs to the meeting hall, formerly a huge loft, where I was to give an opening address. People began entering in small groups. Sitting near the back, I watched the mosaic of familiar and unfamiliar faces entering and smiling to each other. The room filled with some sixty French YWAM workers, the twenty for the conference as well as the local YWAM staff. The meeting began with singing. My heart stirred deeply as I once again sang French songs of adoration to the Lord. I had "cut my teeth" spiritually in the language, and it felt good to worship in it again.

As praise filled the room, I reflected back to those early years when Judi and I first arrived in Europe. During several prayer meetings in preparation for taking my first team into France, we had asked God to show us His heart for this nation—how He saw it spiritually and how to pray for it. I vividly remembered the picture He had given us from Ezekiel 37. God placed Ezekiel in the middle of a valley of dry bones. When he prophesied over the bones at God's command, they came together, bone to bone. Then God told him to prophesy a second time "and the breath came into them, and they came to life, and stood on their feet, an exceedingly great army" (v. 10, NASB). We believed that image represented God's promise for France.

That passage took on greater significance when I began French Ministries in Europe. God put on my heart to find a reservoir of French young people to reach France and the French world. They represented Ezekiel's army to me and became a picture of what God wanted to do. During the seven years I had worked in France and Switzerland, I saw a handful of French young people take up the challenge of missions. When I took my first school outreach trip to West Africa, French Ministries had twenty full-time French and Swiss workers, but I still hadn't seen that army. Now I looked at the French young people around me who were a part of that army. I began to weep as I thought about God's faithfulness in fulfilling His promises.

When it was time for me to speak, I cleared my throat, attempting to swallow the lump I felt. "I don't want to preach, just share from my heart," I began. "During worship I thought about the faithfulness of God to fulfill His promises. It takes time, but God will do it." As I spoke, I sensed that I was lighting the torch of a new generation who would carry it far and carry it high. They were discovering their spiritual roots, and I was discovering the fulfillment of many of my dreams.

Describing the roots of YWAM's ministry in French West Africa, I talked about my personal desire as a nine-year-old to be a missionary there and my first student involvement with YWAM in Europe with the hope of a way to get to Africa as a missionary. I explained the choice that God put before me seventeen years before, when pioneering YWAM's

French Ministries. "I could either go to Africa as a missionary and God would bless me there, or I could remain in Europe and find a reservoir of youth to work all over French West Africa. I decided to renounce my own desires and see this reservoir, this Christian army raised up." Tears ran down my cheeks, and I began to weep. Slowly I continued, "And through this reservoir, to see French West Africa reached with the gospel." Amid more sobs, I took a deep breath and explained, "The reason I am having difficulty speaking is that this morning while looking at you, I realized that I was seeing that reservoir."

Jean-Patrick Perrin, YWAM's director for Mali in French West Africa, prayed out, referring to John 12:24, "Thank you, Lord, that Joe was willing to be a grain of wheat that fell into the earth and died to his own vision, so that You could birth Your vision in us. We are his heritage there."

After several others prayed, I spoke about the nine short-term and ten long-term goals I had set for YWAM's French Ministries at the end of 1973. They included recruiting young people for our outreaches in France, Switzerland, Belgium, and eventually West Africa and Asia; and establishing a farm in Switzerland (which was fulfilled by the Burtigny center), a center outside of Paris (fulfilled by the center in Le Gault-la-Forêt), and a farm in southern France (fulfilled by the Saint-Paul-Trois-Chateaux center) to train and raise up French missionaries. A murmur rose in the group as people realized that many of these goals had already been reached.

"The day before our French school began in October 1974," I continued, "while praying about whether to drive the outreach through the desert to French West Africa, the Lord led me to Isaiah 43–45. In 43:19 the Lord declares He is 'doing a new thing' and 'making a way in the desert.' I knew the Lord was confirming our trip through the Sahara to West Africa." I told how God led me to give French Ministries Europe to Tom Bloomer and move to Ivory Coast to begin our ministry center in M'Pouto. I acknowledged that I didn't understand why God called me there, since nothing remained of what I had planted.

And yet I had reason for hope. I encouraged the French staff and workers that in Isaiah 44:3 God says, "I will pour water on the thirsty land, and streams on the dry ground." I saw France as a thirsty land

and a dry ground. "That qualifies us to cry out to the Lord to pour water upon us and to grab hold of the promise, 'I will pour my Spirit on your offspring.' The Lord goes on to say in Isaiah 45:1–3 that He had anointed Cyrus and would 'subdue nations' and 'open doors before him.' I believe there are Cyruses in this room. God has anointed you to touch the nations." In conclusion I declared, "God is trustworthy. It takes time, but He is faithful to accomplish His Word and fulfill His promises to us. Don't give up. Hold on tightly. God will do it. With patience we will see it happen."

Later that day Isaac Berté from M'Pouto preached and led us in Communion. He ministered with spiritual authority, wisdom, and spiritual perception. I had not seen him in ten years, shortly before Lamine's death. Since then, Isaac had become a pastor and had pioneered five churches in Africa.

After the meeting, Isaac found me in the hallway. "Thank you, Joe, for coming to M'Pouto. It wasn't a lost effort. I know exactly why God brought you there. It was for me. That's how I found Jesus." We embraced and wept in each other's arms. Isaac told me about his desire to reopen a YWAM ministry center in Abidjan, Ivory Coast. Not only were our efforts in Africa not lost, but the reservoir of French-speaking youth was expanding them.

During the conference I listened with emotion and joy as the leaders from French Europe discussed plans to establish ministries all across French-speaking Africa. Ministry teams were already working in Burkina Faso, Cameroon, Mali, Niger, Reunion Island, Senegal, and Togo. Ten centers had opened in seven nations. It was more than I could have ever imagined, and I was excited to be right in the middle of the intercession and planning times.

After the conference I spent a month visiting other YWAM ministries in France. In Saint-Paul-Trois-Chateaux at a YWAM-sponsored praise concert, I met a young woman from the church in Quimper that we had planted sixteen years before. I told her about the coffee bar we started and mentioned the manager of the movie theater across the street. "We prayed so much for him," I said. "I've always wondered what became of him."

"He's my brother-in-law, Yvon," she responded. "My older sister is his wife. She gave her heart to the Lord that summer. He yielded his life to Jesus five years later."

"What? He's a Christian?" I gasped in astonishment.

"Yes," she affirmed. "He's now one of the elders in the church."

Tears pooled in my eyes and hers as the implications of this story and the faithfulness of God sank in.

When the young woman returned home, she told her brother-in-law Yvon about our meeting. A month later I received a letter from Yvon. He wrote, "I was very touched to know that you had had on your heart the man who had worked at the movie theater. I thank the Lord for your prayers and for what God did for me. He reestablished me at every level. In the enclosed picture you can see my little family. I became a Christian in 1977. Since then I have become an elder, the treasurer, and an occasional preacher in the church. God also enabled me to open a chapter of the Full Gospel Businessmen's Fellowship, of which I am president. . . . Thank you again for your prayers. May God bless you. Yvon."

My spirit soared as I read of the transformation that had occurred in Yvon's life. I was filled with even more joy when years later I learned that Yvon was now the pastor of the church.

The Lord encouraged me during that month of visiting different YWAM ministries in France. I didn't hear an audible voice, but I had a growing awareness that God was saying to me, "Come, walk with Me. I want to show you what has become of the grain of wheat you carried that fell to the ground. To you it died. But I planted it, watered it, and brought forth much fruit."

Epilogue

IN FEBRUARY 2007, as I resigned from serving as International Associate Dean of the College of Christian Ministries, I asked the Lord what was next. I sensed Him say my future involved French Ministries once again. Though I had given French Ministries back to God in 1977, He was now inviting me to reconnect with it.

On one Sunday morning in April 2007, I sat next to Judi (all three of our children were grown and gone) in our home church in Kona, Hawaii, listening to our assistant pastor, Rev. Brian Boshard, share a brief message in a kid's worship time. He held up a clear plastic bag and asked the children what was in it. They all shouted at once, "A mango seed." Then he asked, "How many seeds are in a mango?" Since most of the kids loved eating mangoes, they all knowingly shouted, "One!" He smiled and said, "It looks dead, doesn't it? We eat the fruit and throw the seed away." The kids murmured their agreement. "But if you plant it, it will produce a mango tree," he declared. Then he held up the dried, dead-looking seed in the air again and asked, "How many mangoes are in this seed?" Silence. No one had a response. He smiled and said, "Only God knows how many thousands of mangoes will grow on a tree from this single seed."

Sitting there I remembered John 12:24, the scripture God had given me years before when my dream died: "I tell you the truth, unless a kernel of wheat falls to the ground and dies, it remains only a single seed. But if it dies, it produces many seeds." I wondered how many seeds and potential trees were in the seed of my vision that fell to the ground and died. I thought of the many different seeds I had planted overseas. Those who were carrying on the work were like mangoes produced from those seeds. Thinking about the upcoming summer conference in Africa, I anticipated seeing some of those precious "mangoes."

In July 2007 YWAM held a two-week DNA Leadership Conference for all of West Africa, focusing on the roots of our mission as well as the values and characteristics that make us unique. Jean-Patrick Perrin, the new YWAM regional director for West Africa, organized the event. Dust floated in the air that July night as sounds of joy filled the meeting hall in the small town of Koutiala, Mali. Women in colorful outfits crowned with matching headdresses and men in billowy African robes clapped, danced, and praised the Lord in French, English, and Portuguese. Guitars, African drums, and an electric keyboard transported the melody. In attendance were 102 YWAM workers of thirty nationalities laboring in thirteen West African countries. People had come from as far west as Dakar, Senegal; as far north as Timbuktu, Mali; as far south as Abidjan, Ivory Coast; and as far east as Port Harcourt, Nigeria.

One of the faces that caught my eye in the crowd was that of my dear friend Isaac Berté from M'Pouto, whom I had met in 1977. He now served as the director of YWAM for Ivory Coast. Because his country was in a state of civil war and roads were closed, it had taken him three days to complete the one-day trip overland through Ivory Coast to Mali. Along with Isaac were several generations of West African YWAM leaders. I was humbled in the presence of these spiritual sons and grandsons.

One afternoon we spent three and a half hours in ministry, as people responded to the scripture in Daniel 3:17–18 where Shadrach, Meshach, and Abednego declared, "The God we serve is able to save us. . . . But even if he does not . . . we will not serve your gods." The African YWAMers committed to not give up in the struggles to establish what God had called them to. One African couple shared they had lost two newborns in the past five years. Amid sobs, she and her husband declared they would not give in to the enemy's attacks as they ministered in a nation over 90 percent Muslim. Many other people committed to trust God in the difficult times. The service ended with a jubilant time of worship as many danced in joyful freedom. They had sacrificed so much to be first generation African missionaries. Many were misunderstood, particularly because numerous churches believed that Africa was only a place to receive missionaries, not a place from which to send them out.

Alone in my room that night, I reflected back to the time when hepatitis had kept me from returning to ministry in Africa. God had comforted me, saying, "I tell you the truth, unless a kernel of wheat falls to the ground and dies, it remains only a single seed. But if it dies, it produces many seeds" (John 12:24). I had not understood the full meaning of this then. But now clarity came. Precious seeds surrounded me at this conference. God had fulfilled His promise to me from Isaiah 43:4, "I will give men in exchange for you." He wanted to give not one person but a whole generation of young people for the ongoing work in Africa.

A day later I Skyped Judi, sharing with her over the Internet what I was experiencing and understanding. She felt many of my same emotions. "God has been faithful, Joe. He has been fulfilling what He put in your heart many years ago," Judi assured me. "Isn't God good to let you see it personally?" I agreed as we rejoiced together in all that God had done in our lives.

Early on July 13 the leaders gathered at the entry to the hall in Koutiala. It was a festive time, with singing and worship accompanied by guitars and drums. In the Old Testament the children of Israel piled up stones of remembrance as a perpetual testimony to remind future generations of what God had done or of a covenant they had made. In this same light we assembled to plant a fruit-bearing tree as a symbol to future generations of our unity and commitment to each other. After praying for the people surrounding me, I declared in faith, "As this tree grows, it will be a testimony to all who come that we are committed to protect the fruit-bearing seeds—the YWAM missionaries You are planting, Lord, all throughout West Africa." Around the tree we placed stones of protection and painted on them the name of each YWAM center attending the conference. Future generations of African missionaries will see a huge fruit-bearing tree and be reminded of our commitment to each other to be fruitful seeds.

God is still planting seeds. Through the difficult times, He brings to fruition the dreams He puts in our hearts. Though we may not understand how, God is in control, fulfilling His purposes for the nations.

YOU are one of God's fruitful seeds. He will prepare you for what He has called you to. You must radically obey Him. To pioneer, you need to be willing to die to yourself. Death brings forth life. God's ways and timing are often different from what we expect, but He is faithful. Joseph named his second son Ephraim ("twice fruitful"), saying, "It is because God has made me fruitful in the land of my suffering" (Gen. 41:52). God may lead you through the valley and in directions you haven't planned, but if you persevere and don't give up, He will bring you to a place of fulfillment, to the "Promised Land."

There are thousands of unreached people groups, thousands of disadvantaged areas of the world, hundreds of major unevangelized cities, and many needy countries in the world today. Pray to the Lord of the harvest that He will send forth workers. And remember, God often wants us to be an answer to our own prayers. Why don't you join the adventure with Him?

Appendix:
Steps for Pioneering

THE following is an outline of steps for pioneering new missions endeavors or ministries. There are many creative applications for various contexts that can be drawn from these principles. The page numbers correspond to places in this book that demonstrate these steps.

An overall principle: pioneering is a cooperation with God to possess the land He has promised. God works and also sends us out to work.

"The LORD said to Joshua . . . 'I will give you every place where you set your foot. . . . Be strong and courageous, because you will lead these people to inherit the land I swore to their forefathers to give them" (Josh. 1:1, 3, 6).

I. **Before going to your targeted country or people group**
    A. Seek God for direction and confirmation. Be sensitive to God's leading. *(Pages 42, 76, 157)*
    B. Discern God's understanding and will. God desires to reveal His understanding through the discipline of spiritual discernment. Ask God for discernment while ministering and during prayer and intercession times. Have your eyes opened to the *invisible world. (Pages 42–44)*
    C. Research, plan, organize. Find out as much as you can about your target country or people before going. Interview others who have been there. Read material about it. Consider a

fact-finding trip to the area or people before beginning the ministry there. (Prov. 4:7: "get understanding" in all these areas.) *(Pages 77–78, 158)*

D.   Recruit a team to go with you. The coming together of a team can be a confirmation of the right timing to go and launch the ministry. Develop the functioning of the team. *(Pages 153–158)*

E.   Pray for your target country or people. (The battle is the Lord's, not yours.) *(Pages 43–44)*

  1.   Begin intercession/spiritual warfare individually, and then do it with the team.

  2.   Pay attention to what God highlights in prayer.

F.   Begin study of language and culture. It is important to do this before arriving at your pioneering destination, if at all possible. Then continue studying after arrival on field. *(Page 16)*

II.   After arriving at your pioneering destination

A.   Seek God for guidance. Don't just start programs; find out the mind of the Lord and work accordingly (build from the roots up, not from the programs down). Don't try to reproduce what worked elsewhere. Move with what God is revealing. *(Pages 159, 160, 195–196, 199–200, 202, 205, 208–209)*

  1.   Look to and obey God's voice. God has plans and strategies He wants to reveal for spiritual victory. He wants to be involved.

  2.   Fight discouragement in the early days by turning to the Lord and also by reviewing the words of the Lord you have received for being there. Also, encourage your team members when the enemy comes to discourage them. Know well "the condition of your flocks" (Prov. 27:23).

B.   Discern and research the spiritual needs and climate. Adjust to what you find that is different from your preconceived ideas. *(Pages 29, 138, 205–206, 210)*

C.   Learn the language. Understanding the people's language opens up "heart" communication and helps us understand their culture (1 Cor. 14:10–11). *(Page 33)*

D. Get to know and appreciate the local culture. Maintain cultural sensitivity. Recognize that people are people, in spite of cultural differences. *(Pages 29–30, 137, 139, 152)*

E. Work as a team. There is wisdom in a multitude of counselors (Prov. 11:14; 15:22; 24:6). Together discern and evaluate. Make team decisions. Give each team member specific team responsibilities. Work together to accomplish goals. *(Pages 54, 67, 69–71, 72–73, 78, 91, 126)*

F. Schedule time regularly to meet as a team. Plan regular meetings for the team's spiritual nourishment. Minister your gift one to another (1 Pet. 4:10–11). *(Pages 52, 61, 62)*

G. Make time regularly for intercession. God has had plans and desires for nations for generations and centuries. The flow of history relates to the outworking of these plans and desires. When we ask God how to pray for a nation, we are entering into God's purposes in the flow of history. In reality, God is the one trying to get us involved in what has been on His heart for generations. *(Pages 158–161, 197)*

H. Ask God to open your eyes and heart to these people, Ask for His understanding of the country and people, to see them as He sees them. *(Pages 30, 159)*

I. Accept and appreciate cultural and personality differences. *(Pages 21–22)*

   1. Show *forbearance* to one another in love.

   2. God enjoys diversity—look at the way He made creation: colors, textures, a wide array of plants and animals. Cultures are also very diverse, yet God set them in place (Acts 17:26). We can conclude that diversity/differences are good.

J. Establish your spiritual beachhead in that place. The enemy will attack. Stand strong on God's specific Word. God is there. Once you've broken through it, it will go away instantly and completely. *(Pages 107, 133)*

K. Look for a "man of peace" to open doors for you (Matt. 10:11, a worthy person; Luke 10:6, a man of peace). God very often has a seemingly unlikely person there to help you in your first efforts to begin a work. *(Pages 134, 159)*

L.   Go to the people. Begin with prayer walks. Sense God's heart for these people He loves. Recognize the opportunities God reveals for how to begin ministering. *(Pages 62, 69, 161)*

M.   Begin to minister; find an avenue of service (1 Cor. 16:9). *(Pages 96–97, 197–199)*

1.   Do whatever it takes to get in and minister. "Whatever your hand finds to do, do it with all your might" (Eccl. 9:10). The apostle Paul did preaching or tent-making at times, whatever it took to present the gospel.

2.   There is no universal method or type of ministry. Our gifts are intended to serve others, whether by speaking or serving physically (1 Pet. 4:10–11).

3.   Witness. Discern how to present the gospel and begin. "Do the work of an evangelist" (2 Tim. 4:5). We are given the ministry of reconciliation (2 Cor. 5:18–20).

4.   Reach out in love. Don't argue religion; present your friend and savior, Jesus. Demonstrate God's love. "The goodness of God leads you to repentance" (Rom. 2:4 NKJV).

N.   Make efforts to adapt to the reality of the new situation. *(Pages 207–208)*

1.   Adapt as quickly as possible to help lessen the initial culture shock.

2.   Be aware of false expectations. If you have never been to the place before, it is normal to envision what it will be like based on your field of experience, but a new place will never be exactly like you thought it would be. Therefore, be prepared to adjust and adapt to the reality of the situation.

O.   Develop relationships with local churches, if present. *(Pages 63, 68, 124, 134)*

1.   Attend a local church for relationship and for your spiritual nourishment.

2.   Work in cooperation with any existing churches and other mission organizations.

3.   Involve local Christians in the ministry. Cooperate with the local body of Christ. We are not in the battle alone; we are working in the harvest together (John 4:36–38).

4. Recognize it can take three to five years to earn the trust of those around you.

P. Learn from challenges, disappointments, and delays. We learn and grow through difficult times. Ask the question, "What are You trying to teach me, Lord?" Remember 2 Corinthians 1:3–4: "[God] comforts us in all our troubles, so that we can comfort those in any trouble with the comfort we ourselves have received from God." *(Pages 83–84, 89, 93, 110–111, 119–124)*

Q. Be patient; exercise endurance and perseverance. It takes a lot of time to pioneer and establish a work. We possess our "promised land" little by little (Exod. 23:29–30; Deut. 7:22). Pioneering takes endurance: "endure hardship" (2 Tim. 4:5). *(Pages 176–177, 206)*

R. Don't take sides in political, religious, or individual conflicts. There is rarely, if ever, a totally right or totally wrong side. God is above our little conflicts. *(Pages 166, 168, 208)*

S. Send back regular reports to those who have sent you out as a missionary. Encourage their continued prayer for you and the work (Acts 14:27). *(Page 47)*

T. Draw converts into fellowship, discipleship, and ministry. As people come to know the Lord, first draw them into fellowship and discipleship, and then involve them with you in ministry and witnessing. *(Page 62)*

U. Begin to identify and disciple future leaders. Do this while you are doing the work together. Such people are the hope of the future. Without them there is no future. Find faithful, reliable men and women to entrust God's vision, word, and teaching to (2 Tim. 2:2). Beware of personal prejudices. *(Pages 69, 70, 216, 226)*

1. As people grow in maturity, adjust your leadership approach to enable them to take on responsibilities and vision.
2. Encourage them to hear God's voice in the team decision-making process. Encourage them to move in faith.
3. Give them enough room to make mistakes, and stand with them through the process if they do make mistakes.

V. With the help of local Christians and new believers, go deeper in impacting society within the spheres of influence (business, government, media, family, religion, science/technology, arts/entertainment). Ask God to show you which areas He wants you to work in. Then begin the pioneering process again in these spheres of society. *(Pages 73–74)*

W. When the work is established, be prepared to relinquish it. Prepare to be called to another pioneering effort. *(Pages 127–129, 154–155)*

1. The pioneer's skills and giftings are best used in pioneering situations. When a work becomes established, it is time to make room for others with more specialized skills to take over the work and carry it further.

2. Take care in how this transitional process is handled. Don't just abandon the work; rather, transfer or confer it to a qualified person (or people).

Make notes of your own discoveries to pass on to others:

_____
_____
_____
_____
_____
_____
_____
_____
_____
_____
_____
_____
_____
_____
_____
_____
_____
_____
_____
_____

Joe and Judi's engagement, December 1966

Arrival in Luxembourg, 1969 (Joe & Judi, Don & Deyon Stephens, David & Carol Boyd, and Al Akimoff)

Don Stephens witnessing under St. Michel bridge in Paris

*Bible study
at Quimper
coffee bar*

*In the Sahara
(marker post to
right of vans)*

*L: Hotel in
Tamanrasset*

*R: Gérard and
Keith cleaning
carburetors*

*Using the
ladders and
pushing a van
stuck in sand*

*Tuareg boy
("Little Prince")*

First stop sign

L: Tuareg man reading the Gospel of John

R: Baobab tree with "killer bees"

Ministry in village up-country

Two-story house in M'Pouto

Children in village up-country

White trimaran (right) in Papeete Harbor

Khao-I-Dang refugee camp, 1980

Delivering supplies at border

Refugee girls with Lisa's doll

L: Four spiritual generations (Isaac Berté and Joe on right)

R: Planting the seedling in Mali, 2007

Family picture, 2009

Photo by Leah Keith